What people are saying about

We Hear Only Ourselves

First, this book is the beautiful breakthrough of an enormously gifted young philosopher. Then, an original elaboration of the aporias affecting the concept of utopia, after Marx, Bloch, and Jameson. Above all, it demonstrates how decisive the 'narration of blackness', as cast by Fred Moten and Saidiya Hartman, will be for energizing an actual resistance to our catastrophic actuality. On all three accounts, I highly recommend it."
Étienne Balibar, author of *The Philosophy of Marx*

WE HEAR ONLY OURSELVES

UTOPIA, MEMORY, AND RESISTANCE

Bill Cashmore

London, UK
Washington, DC, USA

CollectiveInk

First published by Zero Books, 2023
Zero Books is an imprint of Collective Ink Ltd.,
Unit 11, Shepperton House, 89 Shepperton Road, London, N1 3DF
office@collectiveinkbooks.com
www.collectiveinkbooks.com
www.zero-books.net

For distributor details and how to order please visit the 'Ordering' section
on our website.

Paperback ISBN: 978 1 80341 580 2
eBook ISBN: 978 1 80341 581 9
PCN: 2023938472

A CIP catalogue record for this book is available from the British Library.

Design credit(s): Lapiz Digital Services

UK: Printed and bound by CPI Group (UK) Ltd, Croydon, CR0 4YY
Printed in North America by CPI GPS partners

We operate a distinctive and ethical publishing philosophy in
all areas of our business, from our global network of authors to
production and worldwide distribution.

for b, whoever she is

We hear only ourselves.
For we are gradually becoming blind to the outside [...] But the
note flares out of us, the heard note, not the note itself or its forms.
Yet it shows us our way without alien means, shows us our histor-
ically inner path as a flame in which not the vibrating air but we
ourselves begin to tremble, and throw off our coats.[1]

CONTENTS

ACKNOWLEDGEMENTS

I must first thank all those who have ever taught me: I would not be doing this if it were not for you. From my undergraduate days, I must mention Sarah Bufkin, whose tutorial on Marx made me realise that, fortunately or unfortunately, I wanted to do philosophy for the rest of my life. At CRMEP, I may as well thank everyone in the department. Étienne Balibar has offered so many lessons and so much encouragement, for which I will always be grateful. Most of all, Peter Osborne, whose supervision provided the negativity, in all senses, that I have found I always require.

Secondly, and perhaps even more importantly, I must thank all those who have ever tolerated a conversation with me about this work or any other. Adam, Craig, Anton, Tøger, Millie, Micky; they are all part of this text. I must mention Tøger again, who read and re-read countless versions of the manuscript, and never failed to give critical insight. I must mention Micky again, without whose influence I surely would have lost my mind.

Lastly, I must thank my parents, who have always supported my work in philosophy — with the due amount of mockery. I'll also thank my grandfather, since he is the reason I have my name; he is also the reason I am a communist.

FOREWORD

This book is basically a work of philosophy. I hope that at least one reader is drawn to it not because of a specific interest in philosophy but perhaps because they, like me, think that thinking about our own world requires thinking about a world that goes beyond it. If one thinks this, then a book on utopia may stand out, and perhaps you are that reader. Much of the rest of the book is written with philosophers in mind, so I address this foreword to the reader who I would be most pleased to hear had picked this book out, one whose concerns are not primarily philosophical. Perhaps, even, you are sceptical of works of philosophy and were hesitant to read beyond the first sentence.

The idea for this book comes from three long-standing moral and political commitments of mine. The first is that we are living in the wrong world, and we ought to change it. A lot of philosophy, particularly that which dominates universities in the English-speaking world, has spent a lot of time and effort thinking about what claims about "wrongness" mean. Perhaps that is interesting to some people, but it isn't particularly interesting to me, and this isn't that sort of philosophy. Instead, what I tried to do by writing this book is articulate a way we can think about both the wrongness of our own world and the historical possibility of a better one.

I suppose that is all reliant on my second commitment, a stubborn belief that there *are* things we ought to do. A lot of philosophy is extremely sceptical of these sorts of claims, and it's a scepticism that I share to a degree, but it seems clear to me that there really would be no point in anything if there were not some things that we ought to do. Equally, we would have no need to think about politics if there were not ways things ought to be. There is a lot of philosophy — and a lot of philosophy I like — that I find a little too shaky on this commitment. In some ways, this book is an exasperated attempt to hold onto this commitment while making room for the third one.

This third commitment is that we are all thoroughly and completely part of this world. About a decade ago, it became fashionable to talk about "the Outside", something that we could access, or, in certain formulations, something that could access *us*. One potentially liberating thing about this is that we can look at our world, the wrong world, and feel relief that this is not all that there is, that another world is possible. I do not think this ends up being helpful: the moment we would access something outside of our world, it would become connected to it and thus be just as much a part of this world as we are. If we're going to escape this world, we're going to have to break out from the inside, having been thoroughly formed by that which we attempt to escape.

Those are the stakes. I hope, therefore, that the fact that I tend to think and write in a certain philosophical register will not deter the non-philosophical reader. I should, briefly, say something about why I do choose to write in this way rather than in the more informal mode of address, which I am now using. Broadly, it's that the words we use in everyday life are rather less specific than what is generally required in order to say exactly what we mean in philosophy. We could, instead, try and build that specificity by spending a great deal of time and effort clarifying that we are using rather everyday words in extremely specific ways. That, in my view, ends up being just as confusing and much, much longer. Therefore, in what follows, there is an abundance of technical language, most of which will be unfamiliar to most readers. Immanuel Kant wrote that if the length of books is judged by the length of time it takes to read them rather than the number of pages, then there are certain books that would be shorter were they not so short.[2] I think that this is, in fact, true of almost all works of philosophy.

But I am not just trying to make excuses for what is, probably, a frustratingly inaccessible style of writing that I have inherited from spending too much time in libraries. I want to dispel the idea that your job, as a reader, is to understand what I am getting at, or indeed what any other author is getting at. The experience of not knowing what an author is getting at is perhaps the primary philosophical experience. Surely, no one in the history of reading philosophy has picked up a book and felt that every word made sense with what they already knew. Such an ideal of philosophy is not only a fantasy but also a rather damaging fantasy: unless one thinks that the primary goal of philosophy is articulating, in more specific terms, what "we" already thought, the fact that a work of philosophy does not immediately make sense is necessary if a work of philosophy is to say anything at all. Quite a lot of philosophers do actually think that philosophy is just the refinement of everyday intuition. In fact, if you study philosophy as an undergraduate in the UK, you are likely to hear that "if your writing doesn't make sense to someone who knows nothing about philosophy, then it isn't good writing". I should add that, generally, the sort of person that says this will write in a completely inscrutable fashion about topics that few care about outside of Anglophone academia. In short, this is the idea that philosophy is fundamentally meant to be *comprehensible*. But if philosophy is to serve any radical political purpose whatsoever (as Marx wrote, to change the world rather than merely interpret it), then the initial experience of reading such work must, in fact, be incomprehension.

There is also much to be said about exactly what kind of person is imagined as being able to comprehend all good works of philosophy despite knowing nothing about them beforehand. Here, I am instead more interested in the necessarily accompanying assumption that the aim of reading philosophy should be *comprehension*. Sure, comprehension is an important part of studying philosophy, especially if one is studying for some kind of examination. But we should not be reading with the possibility of an examination in mind, and it is a shame, to say the least, that this impulse seems near-unavoidable. Reading philosophy, just as much as reading fiction, ought to elicit any number of responses. Philosophy is often highly emotional, and there is no good reason to say that an emotional response is a less legitimate response to philosophy. Good philosophy ought to make us do something, or not do something, because it transforms the way we relate to the world. The demand that when we read philosophy we thereby attempt, primarily, to comprehend it, to distill its arguments and conclusion into a "position" that might be compared to other such positions, is a symptom of a culture of reading that requires all its objects to be comparable, exchangeable. It cannot be all that there is to philosophy.

So, if you are approaching this text without familiarity with its terms or, indeed, with any work of philosophy, I would encourage you to resist the student's impulse to comprehend. Of course, it will be helpful to understand the basic story being told, but you don't need to catch all the references as if you were writing an end-of-term paper. Equally, we are used to being assessed *alone*, that one day we will have to sit down, as individual students, and be tested on our knowledge. Resist the temptation to think this way: bother your friends about what you are reading, and think together, even if it's just in sentences exchanged while waiting for a kettle to boil or a pint to be pulled. Most of what I wrote here began that way, and I'd prefer if it were received as such.

I do hope that there is something here for those who are either unfamiliar with or sceptical of philosophy. Ultimately, this book is about always trying, always in vain, to live the right way in a wrong world, and how we could think about a world that would be better. If you can catch even a glimpse of that here, then I will have succeeded in what I set out to do.

INTRODUCTION

This book investigates and attempts to argue for the importance of the idea of utopia in liberatory political philosophy. This is driven by a desire to respond to a rather old question, though one that does not receive direct attention in the course of my argument. This is the question of the possibility of the formation of an agent of liberation in an actuality that appears to be increasingly determined by that which liberation should overcome. One consequence of reading my argument, I hope, will be that it convinces the reader that the idea of utopia is an appropriate candidate for an idea around which to construct a liberatory political theory that is adequate for our situation. As such, though this question is not directly answered, this book may provide a contribution to this most central of challenges in political philosophy.

Why, then, choose utopia as the object of my investigation? It is, after all, almost universally denied: it is always the other who is utopian, in contrast to one's own much more sober, practical political analysis. My thought, basically, is as follows. We live in an increasingly determined, administered world. So the imperative for our thought to remain at extremes, to get as far away from this world as we can, is stronger than ever. As such, utopia, the thought of an entirely other world, is more than appropriate as an object of thought in our theorisation. Indeed, this attempt to revive the idea of utopia is nothing new: the investigation of Bloch's work by Peter Thompson and others in the early twenty-first century was an attempt at such a thing.[3] However, my approach to the problem is rather different from this, since the concept of *narrative* has not yet been brought to bear on utopia, at least not to the degree that I do so here.

I will not try to convince a sceptical reader that the idea of utopia lacks the problems one might suspect it has. In fact, my argument is based around three argumentative moves which accept that the idea of utopia is fraught with aporia and contradiction, but I attempt to work through these aporias rather than show them to be false. Therefore, my argument in some ways follows the structure of Paul Ricœur's *Time and Narrative*, which illustrates the aporetic nature of an idea and, through the concept of narrative, argues that these aporias can receive a response, even if not resolution. By the end, I will show that utopia's contradictions grant it its political force. This world is constantly rippling with negation; trying to find a point of stability would be like trying to keep a boat stationary on the open ocean. So, my strategy is to steer a course that works with, rather than against, the contradictions that make us who we are.

Therefore, Chapter 1 involves an account of the history and vicissitudes of the idea of utopia, tracking its Marxist critique and its reappearance in the twentieth century after Bloch's seminal work. I follow Jameson in dividing utopia's history into two tendencies of program and impulse. However, I show that Jameson's own thought appears to be caught in a contradiction between these two, at one moment appealing to the impulse, at another, to the utopian program. I argue that this contradiction is, in fact, inescapable and unanswerable in the speculative thinking of the idea of utopia. Having made this argument, I argue that the concept of utopian narrative, where narrative is understood through Ricœur's concept of threefold mimesis, can respond to this aporia of program and impulse.

However, the problem only deepens after this response to the first aporia. Chapter 2 therefore attempts to work through the normative aporia of utopian narrative, which is the opposition between utopia's now apparently merely narrative content and its nonetheless necessary normative content. I argue that the concept of utopian memory will be sufficient to respond to this aporia. Having rejected accounts of utopian memory from Ernst Bloch and Herbert Marcuse, I turn to Walter Benjamin's concept of memory. When thought through threefold mimesis, I argue that this will adequately respond to the aporia. I then draw upon Adorno's concept of the shudder in order to account for the refigurative capacity of utopian narrative in the present.

Chapter 3 responds to the final and arguably most problematic aporia for the idea of utopia. In short, this is the claim that utopian narrative must continue to somehow represent utopia's separation from actuality, but can only do so in terms of actuality itself. At this point, the literature I turn to for my argument shifts, as I argue that a concept of utopia has emerged in black radical thought which is apt to answer this aporia. Therefore, I draw on more recent work, from Fred Moten and Saidiya Hartman in particular, to argue that not only is their epistemological problematic of black studies parallel to mine here, but also I am, in fact, attempting to describe much the same thing. I thus argue that there is a tradition of utopia as resistance in black radical thought, and this is the tradition of blackness itself as identified by these two authors. Through the reading of the utopian no-place onto the concept of nothingness found in Moten's work, I argue that utopian narrative can respond to the aporia of actuality and non-actuality only by the testimony to its own non-reconciliation, expressing itself as an impossibility within actuality. Here, I return to Adorno's theory of the artwork in order to argue that utopian narrative will, in fact, be the resistant speech of the object.

In this final account, I hope to have shown that, not merely in spite of but because of its perpetual aporias, the idea of utopia ought to have a place in radical political theory.

I. THE PROBLEM OF UTOPIA: A PASSAGE THROUGH APORIA TO NARRATIVE

a. Utopia's History: Program and Impulse, Program or Impulse

I begin with the distinction that Fredric Jameson draws between the two opposing traditions that descended from Thomas More's *Utopia*.[1] This chapter's argument is structured around that opposition; so an initial, if abstract, typification of the two is in order. The first is the "utopian program", which attempts to formulate a plan for a future society that, if implemented, would eliminate the ills of the present. On this view, utopia is an elsewhere that is not-yet. The second is the "utopian impulse" toward a liberated future which is deemed unknowable at the present moment, but whose traces can be found in a host of our existing practices. Jameson, perhaps rightly, highlights the "obscurity" of this branch of utopian thought, though we will see that this obscurity is essential to the idea of the utopian impulse.[2]

Jameson seems to suggest that these traditions originate in More, because he calls them "lines of descendency" from his text.[3] However, it is not clear what Jameson means by this common origination: the programmatic element is much clearer in the description of the Utopians' society than is any kind of impulse. I argue that we ought to locate the origin of this split within the idea of utopia in the polysemy of the term invented by More. As Miguel Abensour argues, while we know that *topia* is drawn from τόποσ, a place (so utopia is always a location), there is an ambiguity in our reading of the *U*.[4] It might, first, refer to ευ (good), so that utopia is ευτόποσ (the good place); alternatively, *U* might mean "the Greek adverb *ov*, which in front of a single word (τόποζ) forms a sort of unique negative, [...] Ou-topos, the non-place".[5] This latter sense relates closely to the utopian program, insofar as the adverbial nature of the negation *ov* secures the radical separation of this place from actuality, thus this is a complete negation of our actuality. So, Utopia is to be imagined and, later, implemented. The former, *eu-topia* as the good place, corresponds to the utopian impulse, where the goodness of utopia means that our striving in actuality toward goodness is, in a sense, a striving toward this good place. This correspondence is not simple; one cannot straightforwardly read *outopia* onto program and *eutopia* onto impulse. Rather, the correspondence lies between two oppositions: that of *outopia* and *eutopia*, and that of program and impulse. Each opposition relates something outside of actuality (*outopia* or program) to something within actuality (*eutopia* or impulse). The individual terms in each opposition do not correspond to one another except in their parallel opposition.

More's ambiguity here is not a fault, since the idea of utopia gains its critical purchase on actuality in this oscillation between these two possible meanings. The fact that Utopia is a good place that is radically not-here tells us that our society is not the good one. If Utopia was simply the good place, then there is nothing to stop one from writing a book claiming that we already live in Utopia. Similarly, if Utopia were not-here and not also the good place, then there would be nothing to distinguish Utopia from *Dys*topia. Indeed, the Utopians can only make their society free from the ills that More wishes to criticise because they have their own history, radically separated from ours. The critical potential of the idea of utopia is thus necessarily dependent upon the term's polysemy. Given that utopia must always have a critical meaning, lest it become a mere apology for the existent, the very meaning of utopia depends on its polysemic oscillation.

Therefore, since the opposition between the utopian program and the utopian impulse originates in the term's constitutive oscillation, we can say that the two traditions originate not just in More's text but also in his neologism, *Utopia*, itself. Jameson identifies these two traditions though attempts no historical reconstruction of them, as I now will. This reconstruction will show that the aporia of the idea of utopia, not merely the polysemy of the term, is inescapable throughout its history.

i. The Utopian Program and Its Critique

There are two distinctive formal qualities of all utopian programs, which are two sides of the idea of totality. We might, somewhat abstractly, call these *external* and *internal* totality. The former secures the "closure" of the utopian program that allows its radical separation from actuality, which Jameson sometimes calls the "great trench".[6] This refers to the "channel" that More says the founder of the civilization Utopus had "cut fifteen miles wide where the land joined the continent, and thus caused the sea to flow around the country".[7] This closure makes this a self-sufficient totality relative to what exists outside of it; hence my calling it external totality. In contrast, internal totality is a feature of the program that one draws up: it is the total description of the features of these societies. For example, the description of More's Utopia tells us the exact size of the island, the nature of the houses every Utopian lives in, the structure of families, the treatment of criminals, and much more.[8]

This feature of the utopian program is essential to it, for if there were not a utopian equivalent of each of our current institutions, we would not have discovered this utopian program in its totality. This is an "internal" totality, since it shows how every aspect of the utopian society works together with every other aspect.

In the radical tradition, this understanding of utopia is most associated with the "Utopian Socialists" named by Marx and Engels: Saint-Simon, Fourier, and Owen. I do not dwell on their utopias here, as their contributions are not, I suggest, to the formal structure of the idea of utopia that is at issue here. Instead, their contribution is to utopia's content insofar as they attempt to present a society that could achieve ideals of radical equality under specific historical conditions, namely, rapid industrialisation. Fourier's utopia, for example, simply tells us of several "social revolutions" which our world must undergo to establish the utopian society.[9] These are revolutions of passionate attraction, which is "'the drive given by nature, prior to reflection and persistent despite the opposition of reason, duty, prejudice, etc.": crucially, passionate attraction permeates all of nature.[10] Therefore, Fourier establishes revolution as the historical "trench" that radically separates the utopian society from our own. The internal totality of Fourier's system is the famous and fantastical detail with which he described this society: individuals would live in identical "Phalansteries" of 1,620 people, where the exact division of revenues is set out in advance, along with precise descriptions of what these people would eat.[11] Given that passionate attraction is a part of nature, and the social revolution would thus be a natural revolution, Fourier also ventured to describe the changed relation to nature, such that the sorts of fish in the sea would change and the sea would taste of lemonade.[12]

I could add to this discussion references to Saint-Simon and Owen, but, at least for Marx and Engels, these three socialists were all due the same reproach. This is, I suggest, because they took issue with the alleged totality of all such utopian programs, based on a Hegelian argument regarding philosophical method. In the

Introduction to the *Phenomenology*, Hegel argues that any question of knowledge (let's say, "What is Utopia?") must presuppose a particular standard against which such questions are judged. But this standard, the essence of knowing in this form, then becomes a mere assertion and appears as essentially contingent, so

> neither science itself nor anything else has justified itself as the essence or as the in-itself, and without something like that taking place, it seems that no examination can take place at all.[13]

This, broadly, seems true: any pretentions to a universal perspective at any point in history are due a challenge as to why the proclaimed universality is not just universality as understood at that certain historical moment, thus not real universality at all. In Hegelian terms, this former universality is merely *abstract*, whereas a universality created out of the development of consciousness is *concrete*.

Marx and Engels' historical materialist critique of utopian socialism should be seen as a version of this argument. Of course, the dialectical process they describe is a materialist one concerning the development of forces of production, and the relations of production that emerge at particular moments in this development determine forms of consciousness. Therefore, communism must not be an "idea[l] to realize" in the manner of utopian socialism, but rather must "set free the elements of the new society with which old collapsing bourgeois society itself is pregnant".[14] The historical situatedness of human consciousness, and thus philosophy, makes impossible the alleged totality of utopian programs. They cannot be internally totalising, since detailed knowledge of the future that would describe the optimal organisation of society is foreclosed to us as historically situated subjects, rather than having access to transhistorical knowledge of the ideal social organisation; hence Marx's famous ban on "recipes [...] for the cook-shops of the future".[15]

Nor can they truly be externally totalising because such a society does not exist abstractly from its historical conditions of possibility: it is only imaginable once industrialisation has made abundance a real possibility, and society has created an historical agent with the ability to bring about a liberated society.[16] Even in being imagined, the utopian program depends on actuality, since it could never be implemented were it not imagined by actual individuals. Similarly, the utopian socialists' abstract imagining of future societies independent of actuality means there is no examination of the establishment of these societies: "[h]istorical action is to yield to their personal inventive action, historically created conditions of emancipation to fantastic ones".[17]

Since it is key for my later discussion of Jameson's own account of utopia in *Archaeologies of the Future*, I should note that Marx and Engels are not entirely hostile to utopian socialism: these "utopias" retain the *critical* potential that I have described, since "they attack every principle of existing society".[18] Nor does Marx think that the utopian socialists could have gone further than they actually did: "we cannot repudiate these patriarchs of socialism, just as chemists cannot repudiate their forebears the alchemists".[19] For Marx and Engels, the issue with the utopian socialists is that they did not see that their thought was a product of particular historical circumstances, and so the very idea of a utopian program had to be abandoned in favour of a socialism that understood its historical emergence, that was born out of capitalism's contradictions. Therefore, after Marx and Engels's work, "the utopian" becomes "the *merely* utopian": utopia is understood as a bourgeois ideological symptom, whose separation from actuality creates an unbridgeable gap that obfuscates the fact that socialism is really accessible from actuality through the proletariat as its true historical agent. The alleged universality of utopian socialism is thus merely abstract in contrast to the concrete universality of scientific socialism.

ii. The Utopian Impulse
Against this critique of utopia, Ernst Bloch's *The Spirit of Utopia* appears as a radical reversal of the existing tendency in Marxism,

from utopia to science. Indeed, Bloch accepts much of Marx and Engels' critique of utopian socialism. For example, Fourier's prediction that the environment would change to produce friendly animals like "anti-lions" is the object of a sarcastic jibe worthy of Marx himself: "not even hares could arise through mere adaptation to the environment, to say nothing of lions".[21] Bloch's book appears to contain nothing of what was the object of the previous critique of utopia; utopia is far from separated entirely from actuality but is present within actuality itself. However, this is distinct from Marx and Engels' claim that socialism emerges out of capitalism's contradictions. For Bloch, utopia is a "glow deep inside" which directs us toward that "for which it is worthy to live, to be organized, and to have time".[22] The utopian impulse thus takes on an ontological status for Bloch: it is part of the structure of human existence. It originates in our experience's non-coincidence with ourselves, "that I move, that I speak: is not there. Only immediately afterward can I hold it up in front of me".[23] This structural non-coincidence means that we do not know what we are; we only know what we *just were*. This is, therefore, not a merely epistemological gap, but a temporal one. This temporal non-coincidence with ourselves is, for Bloch, "the mainsail into the other world", socialism, since the present impossibility of self-knowledge points toward its solution, which is not-yet: we are "not-yet-conscious" of ourselves.[24] Thus, the questions of "What am I?" and, ultimately, "What are we?" are *inconstruable*, since to construe the question would be, at the least, to say what we mean by "I" or "We". But this is what we cannot do, because of the epistemo-temporal gap between ourselves (the present) and our experience of ourselves (the past). Therefore, the gap between the present and the past is the origin of futurity, the utopian impulse. Therefore,

> to formulate this Self- and We-Problem in everything, the opening, reverberating through the world, of the gates of homecoming, is the ultimate basic principle of utopian philosophy.[25]

While the questions are inconstruable, we continue to ask them: they are "stated but unconstrued".[26] This is the We-problem, whose formulation (with regard to ornaments, pitchers, music, and ultimately, politics) drives the development of Bloch's book and is the basis of utopian politics in the present.

Bloch's philosophy is often referred to as one of "concrete utopia".[27] Therefore, it is striking that Bloch does not use the phrase at all in *The Spirit of Utopia*, only opting for it in *The Principle of Hope*.[28] This is, presumably, to emphasise its distinction from the previous mode of abstract socialist utopias. It is true that the actuality of the utopian moment in the form of the inconstruable question grants it a kind of concreteness; however, given that this is identified in Bloch as a fundamental structure of human knowing that only appears in different historical circumstances, the utopian impulse is not concrete in the sense of being historically produced but rather structures all of humanity from the outset. Where Bloch's version of utopia really diverges from the utopian program is in its denial of the possibility of utopia's separation from actuality via transhistorical knowledge of the good. Instead, what is transhistorical about utopia for Bloch is our *non*-knowledge, our inability to know what we are. This structure will always be historically mediated, but it retains a Kantian stamp of the transhistoricity of human finitude.

I should mention two other versions of the utopian impulse, namely, those of Benjamin and Adorno, though I will pass over them quickly here since their investigation comes later. Though locating Benjamin in this tradition is problematic even before we consider his philosophy itself, since he claimed *The Spirit of Utopia* "exhibits enormous deficiencies",[29] it seems that his objections were more to the version of the utopian impulse in that book, rather than utopia generally. Benjamin was, in his own words, "indebted" to the book.[30] Moreover, utopia is said to have "left its trace in a thousand configurations of life, from enduring edifices to passing fashions", utopia is in our collective unconscious.[31] This unconscious utopianism must surely be understood as Benjamin paying his debt to Bloch, despite his critique. Similarly, Adorno locates utopia in actuality, as that in thought and objects which "is not subsumed under identity".[32] Adorno's relation to utopia is in some senses even more problematic than Benjamin's, so I mention him here only to argue that there is indeed a tradition of the utopian impulse locatable beyond Bloch's book. These two philosophies will be given their due later in this book, predominantly in the next chapter, though Adorno is crucial in the final moves of my argument.

iii. Against Jameson; Jameson against Himself

What is striking in Jameson's work is how often he moves between these two versions of the utopian. At an early point, Jameson characterizes utopia as a "fantasy bribe" in actuality that is always accompanied by an ideological moment.[33] For example, take *The Godfather*. For all its ideological moralism professing that "the deterioration of daily life in the United States today is an ethical rather than an economic matter", the familial connections suggest the possibility of anti-individualistic community that was becoming increasingly difficult in mid-century American capitalism.[34] Here, Jameson is clearly aligning himself with the tradition of the utopian impulse.

However, in later work Jameson calls this tradition "suspicious" in its identification of ill-defined tendencies toward the utopian future, and calls utopia "both a political vision and programme, and a critical and diagnostic instrument".[35] Now, given Jameson's famous pronouncement that "it is easier to imagine the end of the world than to imagine the end of capitalism", which is perhaps a stronger commitment to the unimaginability of a post-capitalist future than even Marx had professed, his utopian programs are not understood to be transhistorically knowable "good places" that ought to be implemented.[36] Rather, for Jameson, at this point the commitment is "not the commitment to a specific machinery or blueprint", as was the case in the utopian programs so far discussed, but "to imagining possible Utopias as such".[37] This gives rise to his praise for his student's *Mars Trilogy*, as Kim Stanley Robinson's work, particularly its first instalment, imagines a "utopian" future which includes "all those bitter disputes around alternative diagnoses of social miseries and the solutions to overcome them".[38] I will come back to this theory of the utopian program as "disruption", but I note here that, undoubtedly, in his work of the early twenty-first century, Jameson works in the tradition of utopian programs.

But Jameson then appears to go back to his previous belief that utopia is located in actuality: the distributive network of Walmart contains the possibility of a future governed by a system of central organisation compatible, at least partly, with the abolition of private property. It is, then, elements of our current society which initiate this utopian "operation" of the imagination of disruptive futures such as Robinson's.[39]

My aim here is not to accuse Jameson of inconsistency, as if that were the problem itself, but rather to illustrate the historical oscillation between the utopian program and impulse: through Marx's critique of the utopian program, Bloch's theory of the utopian impulse, Jameson's critique of the impulse, and then his auto-critique directing himself against the program and once again locating the utopian within actuality. This oscillation, I propose, is constitutive of utopia such that the idea of utopia is located in an unavoidable aporia between the utopian program and the utopian impulse, originating in the terminological oscillation of *eu-topia* and *ou-topia*. There is a truth in Jameson's inability to stick to one of these traditions, but it is one that he does not fully appreciate.

b. Aporetics of Utopia

The rest of this chapter involves a diagnosis of, and an attempted response to, this feature of utopia. Furthermore, the rest of this book deepens this problematic of which we are just beginning to get a sense. I call this problematic the "aporetics of utopia" after Paul Ricœur's "aporia of temporality" described in the three volumes of *Time and Narrative*. This is that the utopian impulse and utopian program "mutually occlude each other to the very extent that they imply each other".[40] Like Ricœur, I argue that narrative provides the only adequate response, however partial, to these aporetics. There are, however, two key differences between Ricœur's argument and my own. Firstly, I refer not to a single aporia that appears in different forms but rather to three separate aporias, the relation between each of which I call an "aporetics". Secondly, my aporetics of utopia makes no attempt at the level of philosophical generality that Ricœur points to in his suggested "ontological answer" to the aporia of temporality, which Peter Osborne notes never arrives.[41] Rather, I hope to show that there is no speculatively non-contradictory account of utopia, and that the idea of a *utopian narrative* should be introduced as a response to its aporias. I will do this by first offering an explanation for how the aporia of utopia is part of the idea itself, examining More's *Utopia* and Bloch's *The Spirit of Utopia* to show that both are beholden to this self-contradiction. Then, I will show how Jameson's account of utopia as disruption, containing antinomies within the utopian program, is inadequate because it does not grapple with the origin of these antinomies in the idea of utopia itself.

The program and the impulse mutually occludes one another. The utopian program, I have argued, emerges out of *ou-topia* as a totality which is both totally imaginable and totally removed from actuality. It follows that utopia cannot on this account be shown to emerge out of actuality, otherwise it would be connected to this actuality and not separate from it. As such, the utopian impulse, insofar as it is always actual, is disallowed according to the utopian program. Similarly, the utopian impulse disallows the utopian program. Historically, we have seen that it was inaugurated by Bloch precisely in response to the unimaginability of the utopian program, the impossibility of such internal totalisation. But even more fundamentally, the utopian impulse is supposed to provide an account of how utopia is a concrete historical possibility rather than an abstract ideal: the utopian impulse says that we do not know what utopia will be except that it is not actuality, but this impulse toward non-actuality is an actual one. Thus, the utopian impulse occludes the utopian program since it says that we do not know what utopia will be, but we do know that it must be accessible from actuality.

But let us see what happens when we attempt to think one of these versions of the idea of utopia without the other. Thomas More's Utopia appears at first to be archetypical of an absolutely *programmatic* utopia. But utopia, in order to appear also as the good place, and not as a mere no-place, requires the claim that "all our actions [...] look toward pleasure as their happiness and final goal".[42] Now, if this were a purely "utopian" idea of happiness, one completely removed from our own, then More's program would not likely fall foul of the aporia I describe here (though it would be problematic, nonetheless, as I will argue in Chapter Three). However, More attempts to give an account of "genuine" pleasures as those which are "according to the behests of nature", and this is always nature as it exists in our own actuality.[43] Therefore, the utopian impulse appears, surreptitiously, as genuine human happiness: only by making this our final goal will we establish utopia, and this happiness exists in actuality as that which accords with nature. Therefore, More's Utopia is only *eu-topia* because of something in actuality, and so its *ou-topia* is not really a self-enclosed abstract nowhere; it requires an actual utopian impulse in order to legitimate itself. Here, the utopian program may occlude the utopian impulse, but it also implies it.

The utopian impulse also implies the utopian program. In a sense, this is easier to show. The utopian impulse is not truly utopian unless it has an idea of the *topos* toward which we are driven. Indeed, even in Bloch's apparently purely impulsive account of utopia, we formulate the problem of the inconstruable question, but "only in respect of what is coming will we be able to recognise what we sought or 'were' before we entered the movements of time".[44] Now, it is true that Bloch merely means to say that we will know the answer to the inconstruable question only after we have arrived at utopia, but the fact that this inconstruability is a *problem* is only such because one thinks that there is a possible situation in which we might be able to construe it. Were there not, then it would simply be a nonsense question, no more a problem in its inconstruability than "how much does the colour green weigh?". The problematic status of the utopian question is made possible by the utopian program, and it seems that Bloch's admission that the question is always relative to a particular image of "what is coming" is a kind of admission of this dependence. One could say, with Jameson, that Bloch did not need to imagine a utopian program toward which the impulse was directed, because the Bolshevik revolution was already in the process of creating one.[45]

Simply, the utopian program cannot be really utopian without relating itself to a utopian impulse, and the utopian impulse is not really utopian unless it points toward a particular program. I said before that the critical purchase of the idea of utopia is achieved in the oscillation between *ou-topia* and *eu-topia*, this oscillation that, at the level of the idea, becomes an aporia. Utopia must be separated from actuality *qua* program (*ou-topia*), but in order also to be the good place (*eu-topia*) it must be good, which must thus be *actually* good if we are to have any kind of epistemological access, however difficult, to what makes it good. Utopia must be both abstract and actual if it is really to be utopia, but it cannot be both.

At this moment, I should mention that Fredric Jameson also argues that utopia is necessarily contradictory (though he prefers to speak of antinomies than aporias). However, for Jameson, the antinomies of utopia are simply the "characterizations of Utopia in opposition to each other", that is, programs opposed to programs, where this antinomy results from the utopian text's difficulty in representing the political as an arena of contestation.[46] According to Jameson, Robinson's *Mars Trilogy* overcomes these difficulties by including a set of contesting utopian programs within this single utopian text: this is Jameson's idea of utopia as disruption. Be that as it may, it does not respond to my argument, since I argue that the idea of utopia is formally aporetic such that any utopian program depends on the utopian impulse, and *vice versa*. Jameson, by contrast, only claims that the content of these utopias is historically always oppositional by virtue of utopia's political import. Therefore, Jameson has no response to the force of my argument here; indeed, I have found no explicit response to this problematic anywhere.

c. Utopia: From a Speculative Aporia to a Narrative Response

I will now attempt to provide a response to this aporia. I oppose the "speculative" here to the "narrative" to distinguish the conditions of adequacy of the two approaches to utopia. The former intends either to describe what utopia would be, in the manner of a program, or to describe what drives us toward a utopian future, in the manner of an impulse. My approach is not beholden to these constraints because a utopian narrative, we will see, does not gain its significance by its ontological import.

One might argue that I have not really avoided speculation because I must at least make speculative claims about the relation of the utopian narrative to actuality for this version of utopia to have any political relevance. I do not deny this: my claim is that we should cease to approach utopia speculatively, not that we should never approach *anything* in such a manner. In fact, one could read my argument as saying that if we want utopia to have speculative relevance, we should approach the idea itself as a narrative feature of a speculative world. I might add that just because speculation and narrative are distinct, this does not preclude elements of each coexisting in the same text.

I now need to reconstruct Paul Ricœur's temporal aporias. I cannot do the wide-ranging and rigorous work of *Time and Narrative* any justice here, but I hope to at least sketch the structure of these aporias in the form that they appear between St Augustine and Aristotle. These are, respectively, representatives of phenomenological time (that time is of the soul, or consciousness) and cosmological time (that time is of the world). Augustine's argument begins with the sceptical argument for the nonbeing of time, that

> the future is not yet, the past is no longer, and the present does not remain. And yet we do speak of time as having being. We say that things to come *will be*, that things past *were*, and that things present *are passing away*.[47]

This is the fundamental aporia of the being and nonbeing of time, which gives rise to the aporia of the measurement of movement: we speak meaningfully of long and short times, but "how can we measure that which does not exist?"[48] This rests on the problem of the relation between an instant and the present. To measure time, we would have to say that we measure some present which exists or a present which once existed, a past, but to do this we would have to say what the present *is*. At this point the sceptical argument seems victorious: surely the only time that is really present is the point-like instant (not this week, not today, not this hour, not this minute…) which must have no duration. If time has no duration, then it cannot be long or short, and so we cannot measure it.

But if we claim that the relation to the past, present, and future is really an adjectival relation where the past and future are modes of the present, namely memory and expectation, then we have the beginnings of a response to this aporia. Time is no longer composed of the present and instant and the non-existent past or future, but a single present in which memory is its past, attention is its present, and expectation is its future. This is the threefold present.

Still, this only helps us resolve the aporia of the being and nonbeing of time; it does not yet help us solve the question of measurement. Any measurement must be "done 'in relation to some measurable period'", so where is this period such that we can measure it?[49] It is of the mind, and what is measured "is neither future things nor past things, but their expectation and their memory".[50] When I recite a poem, as Augustine famously argues, I begin by having its entirety in my expectation, but as I begin, this expectation diminishes and my memory is engaged by the part of that poem I have just recited; all the while my attention is on the part I am currently reciting. So, the present is just what I presently intend, and the present is my acts of attention on things making those expected things into remembered things, making future things past. But the soul remains distended, a *distentio animi*, because these three kinds of action are not the same. The threefold present and the *distentio animi* thus come together to (apparently) solve the aporias of the being and the measurement of time.

But Ricœur is clear that this answer is unsatisfactory: when we say that the future diminishes while the past extends in this *distentio animi*, we are surely still referring to an ordering of things in the world that is not simply of our own creation, our own passing through; Osborne calls this ordering the "serial succession of objective time".[51] There is always an apparently fixed extension of the impressions that will eventually pass through our present, an imperious inevitability over human action. The phenomenological version of time, that of the present, must still refer to an objective succession of instants. Augustine, it seems, still needs Aristotle.

In Aristotle's *Physics*, time is of the world because time belongs to movement, though it is not itself movement. Time is not movement because movement has speed, and time cannot have speed since speed is defined in terms of time, not *vice versa*.[52] But time must be dependent on movement since whenever we claim that time has passed, we always mean also that some movement has occurred, whether it is that of a clock-hand or the placement of Venus in the sky. We would then say that our claims about time are based on noting two points within it (instants) within a continuous field of movement, and thus claiming that one occurs before the other.[53] Thus an instant is a break between a before and an after, and the present is just the instant identified as the "now" by a particular mind. But the present is not merely that which divides a before from an after, it is also that which unites them into a line of succession such that they are to be called the past and the future respectively. The present must secure the continuity of past and future, and it can surely only do this if it is "heavy with the recent past and the near future [...] which at the same time it distinguishes".[54] Therefore, the instant, as a radical separation in the movement of time, cannot, it seems, account for the simultaneously continuous and discontinuous nature of the present, and so it must rely on a phenomenological account of time. But just as it now seems that we cannot have temporal cosmology without temporal phenomenology, the gap between the two appears unbridgeable, since neither has managed to fully encapsulate time. Importantly, this unbridgeable gap means that the two approaches to time are mutually exclusive. In Augustine, the past-future relation is not identical to the before-after relation because the former is always relative to a (threefold) present, which is "an instant indicated by the utterance designating it", resulting in a dialectic between the instant and the present which is foreign to Aristotle.[55]

Before reconstructing the narrative response to this temporal aporia, I want to note some structural similarities between Ricœur's problematic and my own. Not only is he faced with an aporia that appears to receive no speculative answer but also the kernel of this aporia appears similar to my own. We have observed that utopia's ambiguous relation to actuality, that it must both be entirely independent of it and "good" for those that occupy it, is the source of utopia's aporia. Similarly, the aporia at the heart of Ricœur's argument originates in time's simultaneous independence and dependence on consciousness. Utopia, like time, is both totally removed from us, as the utopian program, and yet absolutely dependent on actuality's movement toward it and away from itself, as the utopian impulse. I do not wish to make this correspondence too strict, but we might think that, for example, the problem with both the utopian program and the cosmological theory of time is that they both fail to adequately connect a before to an after: the instant is a kind of Great Trench between a before and after. Again, this is no more than a structural similarity, but it is this mediation between the actual and non-actual that I think the utopian narrative will be able to achieve against previous speculative attempts.

Ricœur's answer to his aporias comes in a "poetic mode" adapted from a reading of Aristotle's *Poetics*.[56] Ultimately, it is that

> time becomes human time to the extent that it is organized after the manner of a narrative; narrative, in turn, is meaningful to the extent that it portrays the features of temporal experience.[57]

Narrative refigures human time via a threefold mimesis such that the two poles of time, both imperious and human, are able to come together in a way that they cannot do in a speculative mode. In the first volume, this appears as follows: $mimesis_1$ is the *prefiguration* of the structure of narrative in the field of human action, its structure of meanings and temporality; $mimesis_2$ is the *configuration* of a plot such that events within it are mediated by the synthesis of the whole followable plot and appear as if they were connected as such; finally, $mimesis_3$ is the *refiguration* of time by this narrative at "the intersection of the world of the text and the world of the hearer or reader", ie its effect on the experience of the reader.[58] Conceptually, $mimesis_2$ is the most critical here, because it mediates the world existing as a field of action and future action after its configuration. Practically, however, $mimesis_3$, the question of how emplotment refigures experience, holds the most weight. This "problem of refiguration" is what leads Ricœur to his long detour on the interweaving between history and fiction, which is, conceptually, a problem of the configuration of narrative. This is why Ricœur's discourse appears to radically change by the end of *Volume 3* into a hermeneutics of historical consciousness. In order to explain the becoming-human of time via narrative's refiguration of experience, Ricœur requires an account of the narrative configuration of time fit for this purpose.

This is accomplished through the "interweaving of history and fiction", whose dynamics occupy almost half of the work, most of

Volume 1 and all of *Volume 2*.[59] I can only state the result of this investigation here, which is that historical and fictional narrative borrow from one another in order to "concretize their respective intentionalities".[60] Historical narrative, we must first note, has a commitment first to describe the past as it actually was. Therefore, in the construction of historical narrative, narrative time, the time of a plot, is reinscribed on universal time, that is, the time of things as they really were. As Ricœur notes, even this thesis fails to escape historical narrative's dependence on fictional narrative. The construction of the historical narrative always inscribes lived time on the time of the world through connectors, like calendars, which allow us "to allocate a particular date [...] to an event that bears the mark of the present and by implication that of the past or the future".[61] This is historical time, which schematizes lived time and the time of the world onto one another through the emplotment along cosmic time, and thus narratively overcomes the speculative aporia of phenomenological and cosmological time.

However, all historical narrative, insofar as it is connected to what happened, is committed in reference to evidence, ultimately, to the *trace* left by the events of the past which are then given these dates. A trace is always a trace of something which is now missing, and it is only in the imaginary ie, fictional, configuration of that missing thing that we are able to reinscribe lived time on the time of the world. Historical narrative thus can only "stand for" the past if it relies on techniques which are quasi-fictive. Furthermore, it is through the configuration of events into a particular narrative, to see "a given series of events *as* tragic, *as* comic, and so on", that historical narrative can refigure the time of the reader.[62] The refiguration of human time by historical time depends, therefore, on fictional configuration for the concretization of its intention.

Similarly, because fictional narratives are always "recounted in the past tense", at least the past tense for the narrative voice, then fictional narratives are quasi-historical.[63] This is something of a problem for the utopian narrative, since utopian narrative is supposed to be in service of a liberated future, but it must always be recounted as if it were past. However, I also take this opportunity to note that it is this interweaving of history and fiction that allows narrative to serve the liberating function that I will argue it ultimately can perform. Fiction recounts things "as if" they were past, and thus recounts "what might have been", and so history's dependence on fiction allows us to retell narratives in order to "free, retrospectively, certain possibilities that were not actualized".[64] I do not want to go as far as to rely on Ricœur's final "hermeneutics of historical consciousness" here, but I will note that, expanding this relation to the level of history, something like the reinterpretation of the past, always mediated by a tradition which serves as the prefiguration of (utopian) narrative configuration, will be a key function of my account of the utopian narrative.

I should say something about the nature of this narrative response to speculative aporias. Etymologically, the English word "aporia" comes from the Ancient Greek, ἀπορία, meaning something similar to the English word, which is itself a conjunction of ἀ-, meaning negation, and πόρος, meaning "passage". Therefore, in calling this chapter a passage from aporia to narrative, I appear to be contradicting myself, and could be accused of misunderstanding the nature of aporia, by attempting to give a passage where there is not one. However, the point here is that utopia's aporias are indissoluble; they will persist no matter what narrative response one provides. Instead, the concept of narrative internalises this self-opposition in part of the structure of the narrative. For example, cosmological and phenomenological time continue to be opposed, but in historical time this opposition appears as the inscription of the latter upon the former, and the appearance of the forces of history as overdetermining human consciousness. With the concept of utopian narrative, I hope, in a sense, to retain utopia's self-opposition, but to work through this opposition such that it appears as revealing of the idea of utopia rather than, as before, making the idea wholly unclear.

With so much ground prepared before its arrival, the utopian narrative should now seem both essential and natural to this discourse. I do not want to claim that utopian narrative stands outside Ricœur's description of narrative; so not only does the above recounting amount to a structural model for my answer to the aporetics of utopia but also it serves the ground of my answer: utopian narrative must be a kind of narrative accomplished all the same via a threefold mimesis, depending upon the interweaving of fiction and history.

The utopian narrative involves mimesis$_1$, the prefiguration of the utopian narrative in a field of human action. How we describe this field depends upon our account of actuality: this could be capitalism, post-coloniality, or whatever else. Importantly, this also includes radical traditions that one wishes to draw upon. As such, there is nothing anti-utopian, on this view, of drawing upon the images of the past in service of the utopian narrative. In fact, there is nothing else we can do; remember that

> Men make their own history, [...] but under circumstances
> directly encountered, given and transmitted from the past.
> The tradition of all the dead generations weighs like a
> nightmare upon the brain of the living.[65]

Of course, this is consistent with Bloch's account of the impossibility of self-knowledge. We always describe ourselves as we were, but even worse than this, the manner of this description is always given to us as part of a tradition of meaning that is, presumably, exactly what we wish to escape.[66] However, the second mimetic activity, that of configuration, might grant us some optimism. In the utopian narrative, configuration involves the work of the utopian imagination (the fictional mode), but also always the organisation of series of events as evidence of a utopian impulse (the historical mode). Now, we can begin to see how the aporia of the utopian program and impulse, when put to work by narrative, becomes the engine of utopia's political force in the present. The utopian narrative reinterprets the past because of the quasi-fictional element of the narrative configuration of our history, locating the utopian impulse within it and thus opening up these potentialities for pursuit. But we can now, happily, connect this utopian impulse to a particular *topos* without the embarrassment of speculatively synthesising the actual with the non-actual: the utopian program is the *end* of this narrative. That is to say, given that all narrative configuration involves the followability of a set of events as a narrative, utopian narrative will be that which shows that, once opened, the liberated potentialities of the past open up new ones in the future. The quasi-historical element of the fictive configuration of utopian programs connects them to the history of the utopian impulse, so we can say that the narrative voice of the utopian program is a future "I" recounting a past of which we are the elements. The trench between utopia and actuality is thus an event in the narrative, emerging from the configurative operation.

The connection to politics comes in the third mimesis. At least one part of the utopian narrative will be its refiguration of human experience such that radical action can take place. Notice, however, that the refiguration of experience by the utopian narrative takes place through the opening up of historical possibilities. But it is in light of these possibilities that we reinterpret the past and compose the opening of utopian narratives. So utopian narratives are not final; each narrative provides the conditions for the writing of another. This is thus a theory of *many* utopias, and so not dissimilar to Jameson, but these are no longer presented as all equally thinkable at once. Rather, they are historically sequential, continually refiguring human experience, and making possible new forms of liberatory political action. It is this refiguration, I submit, that Ricœur means when he refers to utopias as "fictions" that "shape a new reality" by "redescribing life".[67] Not only is this process merely alluded to in Ricœur's lectures on utopia, with a vagueness uncharacteristic of his writing, but also his non-engagement with the history of the utopian impulse means that he fails to see the historical element of all utopian narrative, the history of its impulse, that is always interwoven with these fictions.[68]

Now, some warnings. We should not understand utopian narrative as aiding us by advising as to what could be done in the future, this would make the relation to actuality wholly indeterminate, and would be equally subject to the charges of indeterminacy levelled by Marx and Engels.[69] I also do not mean to suggest that we ought to spend time writing abstract blueprints for the future but to free ourselves of the worry that they could never be implemented; the last thing I want to encourage is more abstract, academic consideration of merely logically "possible worlds".[70] Rather, utopian narrative is interpretative, and any configuration of a utopian program would thus be an interpretation of that which prefigures it, namely, the history of the utopian impulse. If utopian programs are constructed, they will always be constructed as the ending of this narrative.

So, utopian narrative is not subject to quite the same critique given to utopianism by Marx and Engels. This was, at base, that the utopian socialists could not grant their utopias sufficient connection to capitalist actuality since they had no account of how socialism emerges out of this actuality; so the possibility of their society was merely abstract, and instead it should be shown that the potentiality of socialism is, in fact, actual. However, utopian narrative is no ideal to realize: its relation to actuality is not that of the merely possible which must be made actual; it is the relation of interpretation and refiguration described above. This is because utopian narratives are not just functions of abstract imagination but are prefigured by the field of human action, and so their configuration is essentially mediated by actuality.

Utopian narrative thus allows utopia to appear as both program and impulse, and, in the sense that it refigures human experience, it can play a part in the escape from actuality. Nonetheless, utopia is still nowhere; it is not actual, since anything described in such a narrative is configured in a manner borrowed from fiction, which imaginarily draws connections between oppressed pasts and liberated futures. Therefore, this is truly both *eutopia* and *outopia*, the oscillation between which was the origin of the aporia of the utopian program and impulse. This aporia has received a response by the internalising of its opposition in the operation of narrative's threefold mimesis.

However, this answer is only preliminary and, in fact, immediately opens another problematic. That is, if we do not know what utopia is or would be, then what makes a narrative really utopian? That is, how are we to identify the utopian impulse in the past, and how ought we to narrate it? Answering these questions is not merely a matter of clarification but, as I will argue in the next chapter, it opens another moment in the aporetics of utopia: namely, the aporia of normative grounding.

Chapter 1 Notes

[1] Thomas More, *Utopia*, Third edition, (Cambridge: Cambridge University Press, 1551 [2016]). Fredric Jameson, *Archaeologies of the Future: The Desire Called Utopia and Other Science Fictions* (London: Verso, 2005).

[2] Jameson, p.3.

[3] Ibid.

[4] Miguel Abensour, 'Persistent Utopia', *Constellations,* 15 (2008).

[5] Ibid. p.406

[6] Jameson, p.5.

[7] More, p.44

[8] Ibid. pp. 43, 48, 57, 64.

[9] Charles Fourier, *The Theory of the Four Movements* (Cambridge: Cambridge University Press, 1808 [1996]), p.39.

[10] Ibid. p. xvii.

[11] Charles Fourier, *The Utopian Vision of Charles Fourier: Selected Texts on Work, Love and Passionate Attraction* (London: J. Cape, 1972), pp. 250, 67.

[12] Fourier, *The Theory of the Four Movements*, pp. 50, n.d.

[13] Georg Wilhelm Friedrich Hegel, *The Phenomenology of Spirit* (Cambridge: Cambridge University Press, 1807 [2018]), p.55.

[14] Karl Marx, 'The Civil War in France', in *Karl Marx: Selected Writings* ed. by David McLellan (Oxford: Oxford University Press, 1871 [2000]), p.590.

[15] Peter Hudis, *Marx's Concept of the Alternative to Capitalism* (Leiden; Boston: Brill, 2012), p.147.

[16] Karl Marx and Friedrich Engels, 'The Communist Manifesto', in *Karl Marx: Selected Writings* ed. by David McLellan (Oxford: Oxford University Press, 1848 [2000]), p.268.

[17] Ibid.

[18] Ibid. p.269

[19] Karl Marx, 'Political Indifferentism', in *The Political Writings* (London; New York: Verso, 1873 [2019]), p.1015.

[20] Fourier, *The Utopian Vision of Charles Fourier: Selected Texts on Work, Love and Passionate Attraction*, p. xii. Bloch, p.233.

[21] Bloch, p.3.

[22] Ibid. p.7.

[23] Ibid. pp. 206, 192.

[24] Ibid. p.206

[25] Ibid. p.197.

[26] Peter Thompson, 'Introduction', in *The Privatization of Hope: Ernst Bloch and the Future of Utopia, SIC 8,* ed. by Peter Thompson and Slavoj Žižek, (Durham, NC: Duke University Press, 2013).

[27] Ernst Bloch, *The Principle of Hope*, 1, (Oxford: Basil Blackwell, 1954 [1986]).

[28] Walter Benjamin, *The Correspondence of Walter Benjamin, 1910–1940* (Chicago; London: University of Chicago Press, 1994), p.148.

[29] Ibid.

[30] Walter Benjamin, *The Arcades Project* (Cambridge, Mass.; London: Belknap Press, 1982 [1999]), pp. 4–5.

[31] Theodor W. Adorno, *Negative Dialectics* (Frankfurt: Suhrkamp Verlag, 1966 [2001]), p.22.

[32] Fredric Jameson, 'Reification and Utopia in Mass Culture', *Social text,* (1979), 144.

[33] Ibid. p.146.

[34] Jameson, *Archaeologies of the Future: The Desire Called Utopia and Other Science Fictions*, p.4. See also: Fredric Jameson, 'The Politics of Utopia', *New Left Review*, 25 (2004), 38.

[35] Fredric Jameson, 'Future City', *New Left Review*, 21 (2003).

[36] Jameson, *Archaeologies of the Future*, p.217.

[37] Ibid. p.216

[38] Fredric Jameson, *Valences of the Dialectic* (London: Verso, 2009), pp. 410–34.

[39] Paul Ricœur, *Time and Narrative*, 3 (Chicago; London: University of Chicago Press, 1988), p.14.

[40] Paul Ricœur, *Time and Narrative*, 1 (Chicago: University of Chicago Press, 1984), p.84. Peter Osborne, *The Politics of Time: Modernity and Avant-Garde* (London: Verso, 1995), pp. 46–47.

[41] More, p.72.

[42] Ibid.

[43] Bloch, *The Spirit of Utopia*, p. 227

[44] Jameson, *Archaeologies of the Future*, p.3. n.3.

[45] Ibid. p.143.

[46] Ricœur, *Time and Narrative*, 1, p.7.

[47] Ibid. p.8.

[48] Ibid. p.13. Quoting Augustine.

[49] Ibid. p.21.

[50] Osborne, p.49.

[51] Ricœur, *Time and Narrative*, 3, pp. 14–15.

[52] Ibid. p.16.

[53] Ibid. p.21.

[54] Ibid.

[55] Ricœur, *Time and Narrative*, 1, p.66.

[56] Ibid. p.52.

[57] Ibid. p.71.

[58] Paul Ricœur, *Time and Narrative*, 2, (Chicago; London: University of Chicago Press, 1985).

[59] Ricœur, *Time and Narrative*, 3, p.181.

[60] Ibid. p.183.

[61] Ibid. p.185.

[62] Ibid. p.190.

[63] Ibid. pp. 191–92.

[64] Karl Marx, 'The 18th Brumaire of Louis Bonaparte', in *Marx and Engels: Collected Works V. 11,* ed. by Maurice Cornforth, et al. trans. Clemens Dutt, Rodney Livingstone, and Christopher Upward, (London: Lawrence & Wishart, 1852 [2010]), pp. 99–197 (p.103).

[65] I recognise how problematic the introduction of this concept of tradition is here. Indeed, dealing with this problem occupies much of my discussion of Benjamin in the next chapter.

[66] Paul Ricœur, *Lectures on Ideology and Utopia,* (New York: Columbia University Press, 1986), pp. 309–10.

[67] Ricœur only looks at the utopian theories of Mannheim, Fourier, and Saint-Simon.

[68] This, I note, is the strategy pursued in recent analytic defences of utopian socialism. See David Leopold, 'On Marxian Utopophobia', *Journal of the History of Philosophy,* 54 (2016).

[69] See Amanda Beech, Robin Mackay, and James Wiltgen, *Construction Site for Possible Worlds* (Cambridge, MA: MIT Press, 2020).

2. REMEMBERING THE FUTURE: PROBLEMATICS OF UTOPIAN MEMORY

a. The Problem of Normativity

After making a preliminary sketch of some idea, the situation one expects, or rather desires, is that that the next section will be more specific. That is my intention here. However, in the case of utopian narrative, this specificity will come with and by a deepening of the problematic given in the previous chapter. Again, I hope my answer's appeal to narrative will allow me to internalise the aporias of utopia such that their persistence becomes more illuminating than occluding to the question of the place of utopia in radical politics.

I gestured at this aporia at the end of the last chapter, but it requires elucidation. We have here an aporia of normative grounding in the idea of utopia which emerges from the alleged goodness of utopia. In the case of the utopian program, the question of what utopia is seems subordinate to the question of what the good is: one must first answer the "theoretical" question of what goodness is, and then after that ask the "practical" question of what sort of place might best facilitate this goodness. Such an approach is ruled out by Marx and Engels' Hegelian rejection of the utopian program, and I have accepted this criticism. So, one might hope that such a problem does not afflict the idea of utopia once it is understood as the utopian narrative.

This is a false hope. In fact, utopian narrative makes this problem more severe. I have argued that the political import of utopia emerges from mimesis$_3$, the capacity of utopian narrative to refigure human experience so as to open up possibilities in the future. However, insofar as this is an effect of the narrative, one can easily argue that its effect is far too arbitrary to be part of real political consideration. What could it be about any particular narrative that would lead it to have the kind of effect that would play a part in producing this utopian future? Furthermore, we would not even have replaced the utopian program with utopian narrative, but rather would have only pushed the former's question back one step. If utopian narrative is that which helps produce utopia, the utopianism of any particular narrative would only be secured in reference to the production of a utopian program whose nature would need to be determined independently. Now, if the idea I invoke of "producing" utopia appears dubious to the reader, then I am inclined to agree, indeed this dubiousness likely arises from the arbitrariness I describe. So, a vague sense of the idea of production is well-suited for my argument here: certain narratives bring about a series of events which would result in actuality becoming something closer to a society described by a utopian program.

It seems that we have both failed to answer the problems of utopia described in the previous chapter and added another problem, namely, the apparent arbitrariness of utopian narrative, whose reconfigurative indeterminacy would make choosing any particular narrative a matter of instrumental reasoning from narrative means to utopian ends. This would amount to a merely critical capacity of utopian narrative. This criticality of the idea of utopia is well-known. Despite criticising their form, Marx and Engels accept that the works of the utopian socialists "attack every principle of existing society. Hence, they are full of the most valuable materials for the enlightenment of the working class".[1] Here, the imagination of a better society might shine light upon the contingency of an actuality which, as ideology, asserts its necessity. Often, Jameson's utopian philosophy recourses into this criticality, arguing that utopia is a mere "operation calculated to disclose the limits of our own imagination of the future".[2] If this is all utopia is, it cannot be defended against this charge of indeterminacy. What is more, this would fall subject to Marx's charge that attachment to any of these particular utopias would scupper the communist movement, leading to sectarianism rather than commitment to "the real movement".[3]

Conceiving of utopian narratives as those which have a utopian externality (that is, they produce something more directly "utopian") is therefore clearly inadequate. So we might then search for a utopian narrative which is utopian by virtue of its construction. Here, I have in mind Ricœur's modal doubling of narrative into history and fiction. Historical narrative is distinguished from its fictional counterpart by virtue of its commitment to "the reality of the past", and the standard of a historical narrative is measured, at least in part, by how far it succeeds in "standing for" the past.[4] We can call this the epistemological commitment of historical narrative. Fictional narrative has no such commitment; it need not ever appeal to its relation to a prior reality, but rather is preoccupied with its relation to a reader who has not yet approached the text. We might call this the poetic commitment of fictional narrative.

But neither epistemology nor poetics is sufficient to ground the goodness of utopian narrative. That is, it does not appear that any particular relation to the past or to its reader will give us a reason to strive for the construction of such narratives. Utopian narrative must have ethical import, which transcends both epistemology and poetics. So, the utopian quality of these narratives cannot be external to them, lest they are only arbitrarily utopian, nor can this standard be achieved by something internal to the narrative, since narrative standards are never directly ethical. This is the aporia of normative grounding for utopian narrative. I should add that, here, I am not making a quasi-Habermasian argument that utopian narrative requires an ontologically prior normative ground. Rather, the question is how the apparent goodness of utopia, its norm, is to be grounded.

At this point, I submit a hypothesis: the concept of utopian *memory* will respond to this problematic. Utopian memory is utopian by virtue of what it is that is being remembered, inspired by the thought that the past's futures are somehow more radical than ours. By remembering the radicality of the past, we might be able to be more radical in the present. In claiming that the refigurative capacity of this narrative is secured by this narrative's memorial relation to the past, we can say that utopian memory is utopian by virtue of its relating of the past to the future.

I suggest that this is due to what Ricœur calls "the entanglement of memory and imagination".[5] Briefly, the thought here is that memory and imagination appear separate but also inseparable: it is another aporia. This emerges out of ordinary language's ambiguity about whether, when we remember something, we merely have an image of it, in the way we could have an image of anything at all, or whether there is some past *thing* that we are remembering. If remembering is subordinate to imagination, we would adopt the Platonic stance that memory is a present representation of an absent thing: Ricœur calls this recollection, emphasising the *work* of this kind of memory.[6] But on this basic definition, it is remarkably difficult to separate memory, the representation of absent things that were once present, from fantasy, the representation of something that has never been present. Alternatively, emphasising the distinction of memory from imagination draws us down an Aristotelian path, which is "directly characterized as affection (*pathos*)", such that memory is, primarily, *of the past*.[7] Memory, on this Aristotelian view, is defined by its temporal-epistemological relation to the past. We should note here that these two perspectives

32

appear to mirror the distinction between fictional and historical narrative, respectively, where the latter is distinguished from the former by a parallel relation to the past. This entanglement of memory and imagination, I suggest, will eventually allow utopian narrative *qua* utopian memory to secure a relation between past and future which answers the aporia of normative grounding outlined here.

First, however, we ought to address two accounts of utopian memory that might more immediately come to mind: those of Herbert Marcuse and Ernst Bloch. I intend to show that both are inadequate.

b. Two Varieties of Utopian Memory

i. Herbert Marcuse: Erotic Anamnesis

In *Eros and Civilization*, Marcuse transforms the account of social repression in Freud's *Civilization and Its Discontents* in order to provide an account of the continuation of social repression after Western countries' sexual revolution in the mid-twentieth century. Marcuse adopts Freud's argument that society requires some repression of Eros, "the basic instincts of man".[8] But instead of Freud's ontologisation of this repression, whereby effectively all social repression is viewed as a necessary part of human social existence, Marcuse historicises it such that an (undefined) portion of this repression is deemed *surplus*, which is "necessitated by social domination", as opposed to the psychically necessary repression.[9] This maps onto Marx's distinction between necessary and surplus labour, where the latter is made possible by capital's domination over labour but is also the condition of the reproduction of this domination. Instead of Freud's *reality* principle, then, which overcomes the pleasure principle's unabashed search for pleasure and joy with restraint and toil in a necessary process of psychosexual development, Marcuse theorises a *performance* principle, which is a specific historical form of the reality principle's repression.[10]

Overcoming capitalism would thus amount to the liberation of Eros to establish a society free of surplus repression.

Memory, for Marcuse, is an essential part of this process. Adopting the psychoanalytic theory of childhood amnesia, which argues that the phenomenon of our memories not often extending into early childhood is due to the reality principle's repression of the memory of infantile satisfaction. Made social, "the psychoanalytic liberation of memory explodes the rationality of the repressed individual" such that "regression assumes a progressive function".[11] Marcuse attributes this similarity between social and individual repression to Ernest Schachtel, who argues that amnesia covers experience whose remembrance would mean that "man would demand that society affirm and accept the total personality with all its potentialities".[12] This memory is utopian insofar as it reveals the historical possibility of a society of total freedom. Crucially, this memory is connected to Freud's concept of fantasy, where the repression of the drives is cast into the imagination, opposed to reason's restriction of what is real and true. Here, then, we see that fantastic dreams of utopia in the present retain a truth insofar as they are memories of non-repressive life. The amnesia of Eros must be negated: this is *anamnesis*, Platonic recollection, as utopian memory.

However, reading the final chapter of *Eros and Civilization*, we approach what is problematic in Marcuse's account of utopian memory. In a manner that accords with Adorno's claim that the thought of utopia is impossible without "the notion of an unfettered life, freed from death", Marcuse argues that the anticipation of death by the ego means that the freedom of the drives is regarded as impossible.[13] Only in remembering can we enjoy what happened "without the anxiety over its passing [...] thus [giving] it an otherwise impossible duration".[14] Politically, this translates to the overcoming of pain on behalf of the death drive's nirvana principle, the direction toward "constant gratification", which means that death will be approached as a mere fact, but one that we will approach in a way that is more in line with "a truly human existence".[15] Utopian memory is thus the memory of Eros' eternal gratification, restoring it against the surplus repression of actuality's performance principle.

Here, we have the return of the repressed Heideggerianism in Marcuse's account. Marcuse echoes his earlier position that philosophy would "attai[n] its highest meaning" when "everyday existence should once again be brought back to the possibility of authentic, true existing".[16] For Marcuse, the revolutionary act is still about the restoration of a more authentic mode of existence. To be sure, abolishing surplus repression is not the same as returning to the pre-repressed state, since the reality principle would persist after such an abolition; however, what for Marcuse is utopian about this memory is still the restoration of the more authentic mode of existence as the liberation of Eros. So, while the precise nature of civilisation after the abolition of the performance principle is not identical to pre-repressive civilisation, its normative force is drawn from the attempt to find "the lost paradises" of the past, which "are the only true ones" according to Marcuse.[17] Indeed, the transformation of human existence is only ever motivated by the image of a lost, more authentic past.

There are at least two problems with this. One, it fails to do justice to Marcuse's historicisation of Freudian psychoanalysis because it does not seem compatible with the claim that, in historical development, human existence is transformed such that we cannot return *to* what is repressed, even if remembrance marks the return *of* the repressed. After the historical development of the forces of production, humans are surely different from whatever they were in the prehistoric time of the primal horde. Secondly, this regression now seems like a genuinely conservative one, inheriting the conservatism of Heidegger's concept of authenticity. While this liberated state is not equivalent to that of prehistory, what is desirable about it is a return to authenticity, imagined in terms of something lost that must be regained. Indeed, Bloch's critique of anamnesis as the ideologizing of the past against the futurity of utopia appears to be apt here: Marcuse's reading of regression as progression does not allow humanity to imagine itself different than it was ever before in any important normative sense, only appealing to what has already been and restoring that authentic existence, albeit in a different form, to before.[18]

Marcuse's repressed Heideggerianism prevents him from recognising that this memory ought not to understand itself as the recollection of this true humanity, but rather as the construction of a narrative which will not necessarily refigure experience in the image of what is remembered. Both the ahistoricity and the conservatism of Marcuse's account result from an over-optimism regarding memory's ability to accurately present what has come before, unmediated by the actual subject of this memorial activity at a specific historical moment. Therefore, we ought to reject the Marcusian account of utopian memory as anamnesis of non-repressive existence.

ii. Ernst Bloch: Heritage and Red Theft

Ernst Bloch's philosophy of *Ungleichzeitigkeit*, which I follow Peter Osborne in translating as non-sametimeliness, presents another option for an account of utopian memory.[19] It begins from the proposition that "not all people exist in the same Now".[20] Despite everyone existing at the same historical moment, "unsurmounted remnants of older economic being and consciousness" remain as a result of the unequal rate of the development of the productive forces.[21] This is not an idea original to Bloch but is found earlier in the work of (latterly Nazi) art historian Wilhelm Pinder, who wrote that "there is no simple 'present', because every historical 'moment' (*Augenblick*) is experienced by people with their own different senses of historical duration".[21] For Bloch, this theory was used, firstly, for an analysis of National Socialism to explain its appeal by the persistence of non-sametimely elements from barbarism, which appears to be pre-rational existence in Bloch's analysis.[22] The contradictions of capitalist society are thus given a fourfold typology along axes of (non)-sametimeliness and subjectivity/objectivity. I list them here:

(1) Subjectively non-sametimely contradictions are those which result in a "non-desire for the Now", whose denial results in "accumulated rage".[23]

(2) Objectively non-sametimely contradictions are those elements of the forces of production and its corresponding superstructure that persist from a previous moment in their development.

(3) The objectively sametimely contradiction is the existence of the proletariat as a revolutionary class.

(4) The subjectively sametimely contradiction is "the class-conscious revolutionary proletarian".[24]

In the same way that National Socialism turned "red into brown" by harnessing the unwanting for the now that, in Bloch's view, ought to have lent support for communism, Bloch argued that "proletarian hegemony" must be secured by "'mastering' the substance of genuine [non-sametimeliness] and its heterogeneous contradictions".[25] Here, we have an account of utopian memory, which uses the objectively non-sametimely contradictions of archaic consciousnesses to secure the power of the working class. This is a "red theft" of those contradictions, then made brown.

This emphasis on the seizure of non-sametimely contradictions is symptomatic of Bloch's Leninism: just as the vanguard party must seize the power of the state to secure proletarian hegemony, they must also seize these contradictions. Whatever one thinks about the rest of Bloch's account, for example whether he really resolves the problem of a multi-layered temporal dialectic, it will not do for our problem here: the utopian quality of any of these appropriations of non-sametimely contradictions will only ever be secured by their production of utopia, insofar as they lend themselves to the intensification of the utopian impulse. As such, the Leninism of Bloch's *Heritage of Our Times* means that it employs the very means-end reasoning that I have argued we must escape in the theory of utopian narrative, and so it is wholly insufficient for our purposes.

c. Tradition of the Oppressed

So far, these accounts of utopian memory have each failed to adequately respond to the aporia of normative grounding. In Marcuse's version, this failure was due to utopian memory's normativity deriving from its representation of a pre-repressive state that appealed too much to the idyllic character of society before repression. Neither is Marcuse appropriately critical of the mediation of this memory by the subject of this remembrance: that is, he fails to see how the utopian memory is not determined purely by what is remembered but also by those who are today doing the remembering, us. Bloch's failure was in the presenting of the ends of utopian memory, what it is trying to achieve, as entirely external to utopia itself. So, with Bloch, utopian memory is not itself utopian; it is just a memory that may or may not be helpful in achieving a utopia that Bloch already felt he had no problem imagining. The argument throughout the rest of this chapter now moves toward an account of utopian memory, whose normative grounding is found in Walter Benjamin's account of tradition, and I formulate the orientation of utopian memory toward the future, its refiguration, in terms of Adorno's description of "the shudder".

I argue that Walter Benjamin's account of the tradition of the oppressed will provide a version of "utopian memory" that answers the problem of normative grounding. First, however, I ought to acknowledge again how problematic it is to associate Benjamin with utopian thought. In the previous chapter, I noted that, despite his antipathy to Bloch's *The Spirit of Utopia*, Benjamin continued to associate himself with a kind of utopianism. Given that my own account of utopia as narrative emerges from a problematisation of utopia, I am happy to draw upon a thinker who felt that the idea was equally problematic. Therefore, I set off from this quotation:

> [T]he experiences of [a classless] society — as stored in
> the unconscious of the collective — engender, through
> interpenetration with what is new, the utopia that has left
> its trace in a thousand configurations of life, from enduring
> edifices to passing fashions.[26]

So, utopian memory here means the remembrance which attempts "to seize hold of a memory as it flashes up at a moment of danger" and thus locate "the tradition of the oppressed" such that we find these historical traces of a liberated future.[27] This accords with my position that the reinterpretation of the past can reconfigure experience in the present.

That said, Benjamin's relation to the idea of tradition is arguably even more problematic than his relation to utopia. In Benjamin's famous essay on the work of art, he argues that the ubiquity of mechanical reproduction destroys the uniqueness of the work of art and, as such, results in "a tremendous shattering of tradition".[28] Reading this alongside "The Storyteller" reveals that, by "tradition", Benjamin means the possibility of the transmission of experience from one individual to another: the "handing down" of *tradere* from which "tradition" is etymologically derived. Communication of experience is replaced by communication of *information* in the age of global news. Since events are always given to us "shot through with explanation", the listener no longer has the opportunity "to interpret things the way he understands them".[29] So, the ability to participate in this process of storytelling undermines the possibility of the storyteller transmitting their experience to another, and undermining this undermines the very faculty of memory itself, as memory "creates the chain of tradition which passes a happening on from generation to generation", but this creation is no longer possible.[30] Thus, modernity is not characterized merely by the destruction of particular traditions, but of tradition and memory in general, along with the very possibility of historical experience.[31] Therefore, reading a politics of memory in Benjamin as anything other than the destruction of that memory seems difficult.

But this apparent difficulty is mirrored by the ambivalence in Benjamin's work toward the uprooting of tradition that is constitutive of modernity. John McCole notes that Benjamin's attitude toward modernity oscillates between celebration and mourning in a way that initially seems straightforwardly inconsistent.[32] At one moment, Benjamin laments that this all results in an "atrophy of experience",[33] at the next, he claims that the destruction of tradition and memory "emancipates the work of art from its parasitical dependence on ritual".[34] Not only this but also having proclaimed the death of tradition, Benjamin, in the climactic fragments on history, appeals to the tradition of the oppressed as a force in the struggle against fascism. Here, this tradition seems to be part of rather than opposed to the politics of modernity, as a "past charged with the time of the now [...] blasted out of the continuum of history".[35]

The answer to this antinomy of tradition is to be found in the Kabbalistic heritage of Benjamin's concepts of the dialectical image and remembrance. Susan Buck-Morss notes that Benjamin, in his attitude toward tradition, also appears to occupy a tense position between the objectivist "wide-eyed presentation of mere facts" (which mirrors a faith in the value of tradition) and the more subjectivist tendency to present history according to one's political ends (which might presume the value and force of modernity's claim to break with all tradition).[36] For Benjamin, history is encountered in images. But these are not mere "allegorical" images whose meaning is subjectively determined. Rather, they are dialectical images "wherein what has been comes together in a flash with the now to form a constellation. [...] Image is dialectics at a standstill".[37] This, Buck-Morss notes, is an idea inherited from Kabbalistic theology, which reinterprets the sacred texts upon which tradition is grounded precisely to break with this tradition.[38] Kabbalistic interpretation approaches tradition from the messianic standpoint insofar as the monadological fragments it constructs are presented from a transcendent standpoint of redemption. These dialectical images are presented from the standpoint of redemption since this standpoint is outside of history: the constellation of "then" and "now" can only be made by one who takes up a standpoint beyond the "then and now", outside of history. For Jewish theology, there is no redemption within historical time but only outside of it, on judgment day. These images thus claim a "violent expulsion" from history *qua* the handing down of tradition, and so occupy a "caesura in the movement of thought".[39] Tradition, therefore, is broken from without by the reinterpretation of that tradition from this messianic standpoint.

So, despite Benjamin's claim that modernity destroys memory, there is a sense in which a particular form of memory retains importance for him. Benjamin maps these concepts onto Proust's concepts of voluntary and involuntary memory. For Benjamin, the former represents the mere transmission of information, explanations about what has happened in the past, whereas involuntary memory is that which transports one "back to the past", as Proust is transported when he tastes the *madeleine*.[40] Involuntary memory is opposed to its voluntary counterpart, as the latter devalues experience, whereas the former reignites experience by filling it with the time of the now. What is involuntary in the memory is not, of course, the tasting of the madeleine, nor even the construction of a particular "then" opposed in the form of a dialectical image to "now", but rather the refiguration of the experience resulting from the image itself.

We now approach an explanation of Benjamin's claim that the traces of utopia are stored in the unconscious of the collective. Benjamin draws attention to the two forms of memory that correspond to Ricœur's Platonic and Aristotelian forms detailed earlier. Benjamin calls the former *remembrance* [*Eingedenken*], this is a conscious conservation of what has occurred by "giving us the time for organizing the reception of stimuli which we initially lacked": conservation is the work of consciousness.[41] In contrast, memory proper is the shock of the becoming-conscious of an unconscious trace that appears immediately as being *of* some "then", of the past. Insofar as remembrance is the organization of stimuli, it occurs in time, and since memory proper is still a remembering of a particular "then", this is a remembering of a time outside history. This is the struggle of "chronology" against the "heterogeneous, conspicuous fragments [...] remaining within it".[42] One might expect *memory* to be given precedence in Benjamin's messianic historiography, but the opposite is true: "history is [...] a form of remembrance".[43] This is because remembrance is, in that Platonic tradition, a basically imaginative process concerned with the construction of images of the past. But, for Benjamin, the irruption of involuntary memory is the result of a specific remembrance. Just as Kabbalistic interpretation approaches sacred texts from the standpoint of redemption, it must approach them nonetheless, so messianic historiography approaches historical phenomena from this standpoint in order to abolish their "enshrinement as 'heritage'".[44] For Benjamin, the past is not complete because there is a "tradition of catastrophe", which is a tradition of missed opportunities.[45] It is the remembrance of this tradition which I suggest holds the refigurative capacity of utopian narrative, since the irruption of unconscious memory into experience from the empty time of progress might set us on another, liberatory course.

This tradition is the tradition of the oppressed. For Benjamin, remembering the oppressed will make us "realize that it is our task to bring about a real state of emergency", since the after-history of these historical objects of struggle against oppression tell us that their dreams of a liberated future have not yet been fulfilled.[46] This is why Benjamin, seemingly paradoxically, argues that utopia has been left in historical traces: the remembrance of this tradition constructs a constellation of the then and the now that brings to light the catastrophe of the struggle against oppression. But this negativity might refigure experience in the present, since we adopt this messianic standpoint, and are set on another path, after all still in historical time, but now informed by the attempted redemption of the oppressed.

To be sure, this overcomes the Leninist arbitrariness of Bloch's account of utopian memory, since it is by no means arbitrary which phenomena will serve as the object of historical memory; similarly, there is no sense in which we should restore something which came before in order to establish an authentic existence, so it overcomes Marcuse's conservatism. However, it is still not clear what relation we have to this tradition, in what manner we are "nourished by the image of enslaved ancestors".[47] This, I suggest, is to be found in the concept of *debt*. The concept is not found in Benjamin's own writings, but rather in Ricœur's. We often speak of a kind of duty to the past; we must do justice to it: "we are indebted to those who have gone before us for part of what we are".[48] Doing justice to the oppressed and their tradition would mean fulfilling this debt. Therefore, there is a kind of specific configurative constraint on this utopian narrative that says it must attempt to pay its debt, fulfilling a duty which is imposed "on desire from outside" and "[exerts] a constraint experienced [...] as obligation".[49] I will say more about where this debt arises, but for now I will simply note that this account seems to answer the problem of normative grounding. Recall that the problem was that the utopian narrative seemed unable to provide its own standard because such a standard appeared to require being both internal and external to the narrative. Here, we have an understanding of the objects of the narrative which performs this function. The struggle of the oppressed, of victims, can of course never be internal to any narrative: we are only ever given this by traces which are narratively configured, in a mode borrowing from fiction, as being traces of that struggle. But there is still a sense in which this struggle becomes internal to the narrative, insofar as the configuration is obligated to do justice to the victims in that struggle. Thus, the suffering of the past appears to be both internal and external to the narrative. We can see that though the aporia of normative grounding is not eliminated, the move through narrative responds to it: the fact that the real suffering of the past and the suffering as configured by utopian narrative as the tradition of the oppressed are mutually mediating becomes, it would seem, not so much a problem but instead illuminates both.

It might at this point be objected that I have simply presumed another normative standard here, that we ought to do justice to the past, and whether a utopian narrative actually redeems this past is a basically contingent fact about any narrative, and so I have failed to overcome my own problematic. But this objection would be misplaced. I would only require an account of this redemption if the claim was that a redemption in historical time were actually possible. Instead, my argument, following a certain trend in Benjamin, is that the *standpoint* of redemption allows an interruption of empty time via the refiguration of experience in the possible production of a liberated future. The dialectical image that is utopian memory does not catapult us into the eschaton but rather only seemingly does so for a moment by virtue of its configuration, and interrupts that which prefigures it, actuality. Redemption does not occur but rather is negatively related to actuality: it reveals that the past has been a catastrophe, and promises for a moment the possibility of a future without catastrophe.[50] In Osborne's formulation, "Now-time", which is the time produced out of involuntary memory, "configures historical time as a redemptive whole by its mode of interruption (refiguration) of the narrative continuity of its everyday form".[51]

There is thus a normative standard of this utopian narrative; it is our debt to victims in the past. But this does not yet give us any positive prescriptions for action; rather, the prescription is to construct the narrative itself, to remember and thus to let involuntary memory refigure human experience as interruption. There is thus a mediation of the narrative and its other, the victims, as the history of these victims is always constructed by narrative, but their reality always exceeds this narrative. There is no external standard to this narrative apart from those to whom it wants to do justice, and this standard of justice, I will now argue, is not independently grounded by some ethical argument. Rather, it is immanent to the object of utopian narrative, namely, in the promise of a reconciled future given by the tradition of the oppressed.

d. The Future of Utopian Memory: Promise and Shudder

Here, we have what is basically a problem of refiguration. Given the configurative constraint that the obligation to the suffering of the past provides, why does it have a "utopian" capacity of refiguration in the present? What is more, it is not yet clear what relation utopia has to suffering, except perhaps that it is in opposition to all suffering. Here, I turn to Theodor Adorno. We can note at first that, in *Aesthetic Theory*, Adorno subordinates the concept of memory, and arguably the concept of utopia, to that of the *nonexistent*. Simply, our relation to the past and future is structurally similar by virtue of a parallel modal relation: we exist, but the past and future do not. Therefore, any appearance of the past or future is an appearance of the nonexistent. Art, for Adorno, registers "the appearance of the nonexistent as if it existed", which is to say that it bears the possibility of registering both the past and the future.[52] But the point here is not that art will tell us what the future is by its content but rather, "by its form alone art promises what is not; it registers objectively [...] the claim that because the nonexistent appears it must indeed be possible".[53] This is the claim that I must now elucidate, but before doing so I want to note one quotation which draws Adorno remarkably close to Benjamin on this issue, and makes clear the relevance of Adorno's argument to my project. The nonexistent's "claim to existence flickers out in aesthetic semblance; yet what does not exist, by appearing, is promised. *The constellation of the existing and nonexisting is the utopic figure of art*".[54] I submit that, in this regard, what Adorno says is true of art is true of utopian narrative.

Adorno's claim is that art gains an illusory completeness of autonomy that, though illusory, thereby gives it a kind of real autonomy. For Adorno, aesthetic autonomy is akin to autonomy in Kant's practical philosophy, that is, art appears as a self-legislating subject.[55] If we transpose Kant's transcendental subject to society, a typical post-Hegelian move, we can say that art's autonomy is socially determined just as Kantian autonomy is transcendentally-subjectively determined. This allows Adorno to argue that art's sociality, despite being socially determined, "a *fait social*", appears under the capitalist mode of production as that of the artist creating separately to society, rather than at the behest of institutions (e.g., the church or the monarchy).[56] So, in bourgeois society, art is socially determined as opposition to society. Crucially, it opposes the totalising domination of the same, the principle of exchange. By appearing as socially useless, it appears to have no use-value and so cannot be subordinated to purely quantitative exchange-value. This is the dual character of art in Adorno's *Aesthetic Theory*, drawing from the dual character of the commodity in Marx's *Capital*, as use- and exchange-value.

However, there is no purely autonomous art: it must still be produced and so still depends on the mode of production. Autonomous art is that where the autonomous takes priority over the heteronomous by virtue of its construction or, we might say, its configuration. But the artwork presents itself as totally autonomous: often, when confronted with some artwork, it appears opposed to exchange because it appears as if it were the product of a process which is independent of society. One should not view this illusory autonomy as a deficiency of the artwork, but rather the fact that it appears as an illusion criticises the impossibility of freedom within actuality. The artwork thus appears as the appearance of a nonexistent freedom, but constructs this out of a constellation between this freedom and the determination of the existent. The illusory autonomy of the artwork thus promises a reconciled future, even happiness itself, but its truth is not in the making of the promise but in the fact that it reveals the fact that this promise is always broken.[57] This utopian promise is a promise of reconciliation, one "of a condition beyond the diremption of the individual and collective".[58] In allowing its various socially determined parts to appear to come together as a whole, the artwork prefigures a utopian society by modelling "the 'belonging together' of the one and the many".[59] We thus have a futurity of the *promise* in Adorno's theory of the artwork.

We must now bring this account to bear on that of utopian memory drawn from Benjamin. In comparison to Benjamin's work, the concept of memory is comparatively scarce in Adorno's writing. Significantly, however, Adorno chooses to end the work with a reference to a kind of tradition of the oppressed, asking "what would art be, as the writing of history, if it shook off the memory of accumulated suffering".[60] This suffering is the fact that art is a thing rather than the autonomous subject that it illusorily presents itself to be; it suffers under its continual domination.[61] Similarly, the suffering of the individuals of the past is the domination which appears as a catastrophe of the struggle against that domination, the unfulfilled promise of happiness. Artworks only have their truth, which is this utopian promise of reconciliation, when their configuration reflects the history of artwork as the continual *failure* to make good on that promise. Artworks are bound by a duty to do justice to the past in remembering the liberation promised in that past, only then do they reflect their social character and gain their truth in this promise. It is the debt to the past's unfulfilled promise of reconciliation that would therefore give a particular memory its utopian quality, rather than an abstract debt of "justice".

Utopian narrative is thus immanently constructed as utopian via the dialectic of debt and promise: we configure a memory of the past's future, and this future promised reconciliation which it has failed to provide, so we are indebted to the past by virtue of this failure. Such configuration has, then, the refigurative capacity of the promise of a reconciled future in the present, of which we know little except that it is as yet unfulfilled. This accords well with Adorno's account of tradition, which might act as a summary of this stage in the argument:

> Whoever seeks to avoid betraying the bliss which tradition
> still promises in some of its images and the possibilities
> buried beneath its ruins must abandon that tradition which
> turns possibilities and meanings into lies.[62]

Therefore, we have a standard of utopian narrative that is both non-arbitrary and immanently ethical. It is non-arbitrary because our debt to the suffering of the past is not arbitrary, though that suffering always exceeds the narrative. This debt is ethical because we are the future of the past and thus bound by the unfulfilled promise made by the future to the oppressed in the past; it is *immanently* ethical because the ethicality is contained within the narrative as this dialectic of debt and promise. We now have an ethico-temporal coding of the past and the future as debt and promise respectively, a kind of temporal obligation.

At this point, I want to distinguish this account of debt and promise from the post-Heideggerian legacy found in Derrida's later work. According to Derrida, who follows Heidegger in emphasising that historical being is "inherited": "an inheritance is always the reaffirmation of a debt".[63] But Derrida wishes to break with this necessary reaffirmation, with "a promise of a gift beyond exchange", that is the emancipatory promise of a people-to come.[64] In a typical Derridean argument, debt itself promises a future emancipated from debt, as it includes its own constitutive exclusion. The promise could be construed as utopian, despite Derrida's eschewing of the term in "Marx and Sons".[65] Importantly, it is likely that Ricœur's concept of debt, which first motivated me to introduce it, is drawn from the same Heideggerian inheritance. Nonetheless, my concept of debt here is rather different from Derrida's. On my account, utopian narrative has a debt that does not arise from our actual historical inheritance but from the fact that there is a tradition of *suffering*. Furthermore, it is the fact of this suffering, not the structure of debt, that registers the utopian promise on my argument. Equally, Derrida's notion of the *promise* is not the same as mine here. In Derrida, its force is contained in the real fulfilment of that promise:

> [T]he effectivity or actuality of the democratic promise, like that of the communist promise, will always keep within it, and it must do so, this absolutely undetermined mesianic [sic.] hope at its heart.[66]

But on my account, the promise only gains political force in the reminder that it has been broken and will always continue to be broken, since it is only an illusory promise created by the configuration of utopian narrative. Remember, this promise is always an imaginative construction, thus its refigurative capacity is that it broadens the horizon of expectation in its perpetual brokenness. There are thus three problems with this Derridean view for our purposes here, that I can only sketch. Firstly, the affirmation of the emancipatory promise all too easily slides into the ideological affirmation of the existent: if the promise is already here, then there is a sense in which our consciousness is already the right one. Secondly, we have already said that utopia is radically separated from actuality, motivated by the thought that there is nothing right in this world, and thus any connection to a real promise in the existent would fail to be properly utopian. Finally, the reality of the Derridean promise would make its incorporation into a theory of utopian *narrative* all too difficult, by virtue of the ontological commitment required by the analysis of gift-exchange and inheritance out of which Derrida's promise arises.

Though I have detailed the mode of configuration of utopian narrative on my account and distinguished it from a similar account, I have yet to make good on my promise to speak of the refigurative capacity of utopian narrative in actuality. I will now do so explicitly via the concept of the *shudder* that one finds in Adorno. Note that the term appears to be borrowed from Bloch, who speaks of "the shudder of the absolute question" as a phenomenological response to the asking of the inconstruable question.[67] Therefore, we ought to read the shudder as a key part of the (idiosyncratically negative) utopianism in Adorno.

The shudder is double-coded in Adorno's writing: the artwork "shudders at" society, but the shudder is also a kind of experience of the subject.[68] Let us start with the latter. The shudder begins, in human pre-history, as the primordial response to a materiality entirely beyond the human individual: it is a chill of anxiety when watching a storm roll in, or hearing the call of a predator in the distance. This shudder survives in the artwork as the recollection of this initial shudder, this confrontation by something entirely other. The artwork's autonomy is a practical autonomy; it appears like a self-legislating subject, and so our reaction is that of being "overwhelmed" by their appearance of action: "to this extent they are truly afterimages of the primordial shudder".[69]

In the case of the former, the artwork's illusory autonomy allows it to shudder "at" society as a rejection of it. Two things are worth saying here. Firstly, Adorno's phrase in German is "*vor der ihr schaudert*", where "*vor*" could be translated as "before" or "from" and, as here, "at".[70] So we should not read this shudder as an intentional phenomenological structure, in the Husserlian sense of a consciousness directed "at" some object. Instead, the shudder is "at" something in the sense of a response to that with which one is confronted. So, the artwork shudders at society in the sense that its illusory autonomy is opposed to determinate society; the artwork's configuration as autonomous is a resistance to the heteronomous actuality which prefigures it.

Second, this shudder is only illusory since the artwork's autonomy is an illusory semblance. But again, it is this semblance which provides the artwork's political force. We shudder at the autonomy of the artwork in a momentary "liquidation of the I", recognising for a moment that the autonomous "I" we take ourselves to be is, under conditions of domination, as illusory as the autonomy of the artwork: "[the I] itself is not ultimate, but semblance".[71] The shudder is thus the appearance of our own materiality.

So, the illusion of the completion of the artwork serves as a model of reconciliation; but the falsity of this reconciliation, the broken promise, enacts a momentary liquidation of who we are, opening up expectation to realise that this liquidation could occur, since "the shudder feels the potential as if it were actual".[72] This liquidation of the I would amount to the final reconciliation between the I and materiality, which is precisely that reconciliation promised by the utopian narrative. Remembering the shudder as the confrontation of the individual by its first other is the dialectical opposite of remembering the suffering of the past, since this suffering is the domination of the other over the individual. In the artwork's utopian memory, the shudder becomes not the confrontation of the individual by an opposed materiality but the confrontation of the I by its own materiality. The shudder is thus the refigurative force of utopian memory that provides the possibility of a politics informed by utopian narrative.

The reader might have noticed that while Benjamin's account of memory and tradition is relatively easily transferable onto the concept of narrative, it is less easy to do so in the case of Adorno's theory of the artwork. Indeed, I want to avoid any bold claim as to the identity of narrative and the artwork. My claim is more modest: there is much of what Adorno says of the artwork that is true of narrative, and, indeed, the utopian elements of the artwork accord well with what makes a particular narrative utopian. It is true that I have had to give a reading of Adorno's theory of the artwork in terms of (utopian) narrative in order to bring the former to bear on the latter, but I only do so in the sense that, amongst other things, artworks can be understood as a threefold mimesis of action. They are prefigured by the field of human action, they configure heterogeneous parts to construct a semblance of autonomous action, and they refigure human experience in the shudder. There is surely more to artworks than this, but this minimal claim, which I hope to have shown in the previous pages, is all that is required for my argument.

e. Threefold Mimesis Revisited

Let me recapitulate the account of utopian narrative at which we have arrived. All utopian narrative is prefigured by the apparent continuity of daily life that we call tradition, that each event is the result of a handing down from previous events. While the Benjaminian aspect of my account might appear to disallow an appeal to the force of tradition, modernity is not a single event which breaks with all tradition, but is rather the continual breaking which must be prefigured by a tradition lest it have nothing left to break. The configuration of the utopian narrative is of a memory of the suffering of the past, constructing, from the standpoint of redemption, a constellation between now and then by a remembrance of that tradition which causes the unconscious broken promises of the past to flash up in the present. Utopian memory is ethically bound to this remembrance of that suffering by virtue of the past's unfulfilled promises, which produces an ethical imperative in the present, a debt. This configuration on the basis of debt results in the illusion of reconciliation, an ultimately unfulfilled promise in the present. I should note, therefore, that the promise of utopian narrative in the present is modally different from the broken promises of the past. Rather, the latter only operates as the source of the obligation to configure a narrative which would produce the former. Utopian narratives work by identifying the promises and recognising that they have been broken, reigniting a utopian futurity in general in the present. I stress that this reinterpretation of the past is not in service of an education whereby we would learn from and attempt to reignite the past's more radical futures.

This leads us to the refigurative capacity of utopian narrative. This required an account of the phenomenological operation that this narrative would accomplish. I have mediated a great deal of this through Adorno's specific theory of the artwork, but my claim here is that insofar as artworks are a remembrance of the shudder as the experience of domination, they are utopian narratives *qua* utopian memory. The refigurative capacity of utopian narrative is therefore the recognition of the broken promise of reconciliation in the shudder. In its configuration, the utopian narrative shudders at the tradition of suffering it describes, where this tradition is also a tradition of shuddering, and this semblance of the artwork's shuddering momentarily reveals that the "I" is also semblance. The utopian narrative, at least for a moment, allows us to experience what it would mean to be utopian, that is, to break with everything we are and everything that is actual.

At the end of this chapter, we reach an account of utopian narrative that not only overcomes the aporia of normativity with which we opened but also immanently connects to a utopian politics of radical separation. However, we are by no means finished with the aporias of utopia. Utopian narrative must somehow narrate the promises of the past, but insofar as these are unfulfilled promises, they are the promises of a break with actuality. So now we approach the problem of how to narrate this break, since such a break must be articulable in terms intelligible in our present actuality. That is, utopian narrative is always negatively mediated by the actuality it seeks to escape and thus an affirmation of its separation, utopia's impossibility within actuality, is always in danger of obscuring this mediation and thus confusing the "imagined" with the "potential — that is, the *already actually possible*".[73] In short, utopia must be radically separated from actuality but also must always be articulable in terms of actuality, if it is to retain its critical potential. The next chapter is concerned with answering this aporia of actuality and non-actuality.

Chapter 2 Notes

[1] Marx and Engels, p.269.

[2] Jameson, *Valences of the Dialectic*, p.413.

[3] Karl Marx and Friedrich Engels, 'The Alleged Splits in the International', in *The Political Writings* (London; New York: Verso, 1872 [2019]), pp. 982–83.

[4] Ricœur, *Time and Narrative*, 3, p.142.

[5] Paul Ricœur, *Memory, History, Forgetting* (Chicago: University of Chicago Press, 2004), p.7.

[6] Ibid. p.15.

[7] Ibid.

[8] Herbert Marcuse, *Eros and Civilization: A Philosophical Inquiry into Freud* (London: Allen Lane, The Penguin Press, 1955 [1969]), p.11.

[9] Ibid. p.35.

[10] Ibid.

[11] Ibid. p.19.

[12] Ernest G Schachtel, 'On Memory and Childhood Amnesia', *Psychiatry*, 10 (1947), 24.

[13] Ernst Bloch, *The Utopian Function of Art and Literature: Selected Essays* (MIT Press, 1989), p.10.

[14] Marcuse, p.233.

[15] Ibid. pp. 234–35.

[16] Herbert Marcuse, 'Contributions to a Phenomenology of Historical Materialism', in *Heideggerian Marxism,* ed. by John Abromeit and Richard Wolin, trans. Eric Oberle (Lincoln, NE: University of Nebraska Press, 1928 [2005]), p.15.

[17] Marcuse, *Eros and Civilization: A Philosophical Inquiry into Freud,* p.233.

[18] Bloch, *The Principle of Hope,* 1, p.140.

[19] Peter Osborne, 'Out of Sync: Tomba's Marx and the Problem of a Multi-Layered Temporal Dialectic', *Historical Materialism,* 23 (2015).

[20] Ernst Bloch, *Heritage of Our Times* (Oxford: Polity, 1935 [1990]), p.97.

[21] Ibid. p.106.

[22] Quoted in Fredric J. Schwartz, 'Ernst Bloch and Wilhelm Pinder: Out of Sync', *Grey Room* (2001), 62.

[23] Bloch, *Heritage of Our Times,* p.107.

[24] Ibid. p.108. The German word here translated as "non-desire" is Bloch's construction *nichtwollen*. The translation is unhelpful, because it suggests that Bloch is introducing a quasi-psychoanalytic category. There are two reasons to think that this is not what he is doing. Firstly, what might be read as "desire" in Freud's work is not *Wolle* but *Wunsch*, whose meaning is closer to "wish" than the former's "want". Secondly, *"nichtwollen"* is a nominalisation of the verbal phrase "nicht wollen," and so is closer in meaning to an English gerund; so "unwanting" is a much better translation. On this reading, *Nichtwollen* appears less a spurious psychoanalytic concept and more a simple not-wanting of the Now. It is sometimes translated as "unwillingness", which, though introducing yet another category, that of the will, is also a better translation than non-desire. Ernst Bloch, *Erbschaft Dieser Zeit* (Frankfurt am Main: Suhrkamp Verlag, 1935), p.81.

[25] Ibid. pp. 72, 114.

[26] Walter Benjamin, 'Paris, the Capital of the Nineteenth Century', in *The Arcades Project,* ed. by Rolf Tiedemann, trans. Howard Eiland and Kevin McLaughlin (Cambridge, Massachusetts; London: Belknap Press, 1935 [1999]), pp. 4–5.

[27] Walter Benjamin, 'Theses on the Philosophy of History', in *Illuminations,* ed. by Hannah Arendt, trans. Harry Zohn (London: Fontana, 1940 [1973]), pp. 247–48.

[28] Walter Benjamin, 'The Work of Art in the Age of Mechanical Reproduction', in *Illuminations,* ed. by Hannah Arendt, trans. Harry Zohn (London: Fontana, 1936 [1973]), p. 215.

[29] Benjamin, 'The Storyteller', p.89.

[30] Ibid. p.97.

[31] Osborne, *The Politics of Time: Modernity and Avant-Garde*, p.135.

[32] John McCole, *Walter Benjamin and the Antinomies of Tradition* (Ithaca; London: Cornell University Press, 1993), pp. 2–3.

[33] Walter Benjamin, 'On Some Motifs in Baudelaire', in *Illuminations,* ed. by Hannah Arendt (London: Fontana, 1939 [1973]), p.155.

[34] Benjamin, 'The Work of Art in the Age of Mechanical Reproduction', p.218.

[35] Benjamin, 'Theses on the Philosophy of History', p.253.

[36] Susan Buck-Morss, *Dialectics of Seeing: Walter Benjamin and the Arcades Project* (Cambridge, Mass; London: MIT Press, 1989), p.228.

[37] Benjamin, *The Arcades Project*, pp. N2a,3.

[38] Buck-Morss, p.233.

[39] Benjamin, *The Arcades Project*, pp. N10a,3.

[40] Benjamin, 'On Some Motifs in Baudelaire', p.154.

[41] Ibid. p.158. Quoting Paul Valéry.

[42] Ibid. p.181.

[43] Benjamin, *The Arcades Project*, pp. N8,1.

[44] Ibid. pp. N9,4.

[45] Ibid. pp. N9a,1.

[46] Benjamin, 'Theses on the Philosophy of History', p.248. This notion of after-history emerges out of the "Epistemo-Critical Foreword" to Benjamin's essay on German tragic drama: *Origin of the German Trauerspiel,* (Cambridge, MA; London: Harvard University Press, 1928 [2019]). It emerges again in Benjamin's account of the monadological structure of historical objects in *The Arcades Project*. N10,3.

[47] Benjamin, 'Theses on the Philosophy of History', p.252.

[48] Ricœur, *Memory, History, Forgetting*, p.89.

[49] Ibid. p.88.

[50] Osborne, *The Politics of Time: Modernity and Avant-Garde*, p.153. The diagram on this page is particularly helpful in bringing this problem out.

[51] Ibid. p.156.

[52] Theodor W. Adorno, *Aesthetic Theory*, (London: Bloomsbury Academic, 1970 [2014]), p.114.

[53] Ibid.

[54] Ibid. p.318. My emphasis.

[55] Immanuel Kant, 'Groundwork for the Metaphysics of Morals', in *Practical Philosophy*, edited and translated by Mary J. Gregor (Cambridge: Cambridge University Press, 1785 [1999]), p. 4:447.

[56] Adorno, *Aesthetic Theory*, p.308.

[57] Ibid. p.114.

[58] Ibid. p.179.

[59] Peter Osborne, 'Theorem 4: Autonomy: Can It Be True of Art and Politics at the Same Time?', *Open: Cahier on Art and the Public Domain*, 23 (2012), 5.

[60] Adorno, *Aesthetic Theory*, p.352.

[61] Ibid. p.100.

[62] Theodor W. Adorno, 'On Tradition', *Telos*, 1992 (1966 [1992]), 82.

[63] Martin Heidegger, *Being and Time* (San Francisco: Harper and Row, 1927 [1962]), p.435.

[64] Jacques Derrida, *Specters of Marx: The State of the Debt, the Work of Mourning, and the New International* (New York; London: Routledge, 1993 [2006]), p.201.

[65] Jacques Derrida, 'Marx and Sons', in *Ghostly Demarcations: A Symposium on Jacques Derrida's Spectres of Marx*, ed. by Michael Sprinker, trans. G. M. Goshgarian (London: Verso, 1999 [2008]).

[66] Derrida, *Specters of Marx: The State of the Debt, the Work of Mourning, and the New International*, p.81.

[67] Bloch, *The Spirit of Utopia*, p.229.

[68] Adorno, *Aesthetic Theory*, pp. 308, 33.

[69] Ibid. p.111.

[70] Theodor W. Adorno, *Ästhetische Theorie* (Berlin: De Gruyter, 1970 [2021]), p.215.

[71] Adorno, *Aesthetic Theory*, p.333.

[72] Ibid.

[73] Peter Osborne, 'The Dreambird of Experience: Utopia, Possibility, Boredom', *Radical philosophy*, 137 (2006), 36. Emphasis in original.

3. NARRATING THE IMPOSSIBLE

a. The Aporia of (Non-)Actuality: Toward Black Radical Thought

The analysis of utopian narrative is a kind of reworking of the idea of utopian impulse. It is the narration of a history of suffering such that human experience is refigured to shudder against actuality, apparently driving us away from an oppressed present to a liberated future. But what animated this whole endeavour was the terminological oscillation between *outopia* and *eutopia* that is constitutive of utopia's meaning. The point of the utopian narrative was to internalise the aporia generated from this oscillation, such that both utopia's radical separation from actuality and its goodness could be sustained. However, by connecting the utopian narrative to a historical narrative of suffering, we appear to have done away with this radical separation, in favour of an idea of utopian narrative that is seemingly compatible with a mere improvement within actuality. That is, there is nothing in the concept of utopian narrative described in the previous chapter that says our actuality could not be somehow connected to utopia.

This seems to be a clear abandonment of the idea of utopia, since it is not a strictly *utopian* narrative, rather only one concerning liberation in general. In this mode, "utopian" narrative risks becoming ideological insofar as it affirms the possibility of achieving this liberation within actuality. As such, a genuinely utopian narrative must assert its incompatibility with actuality and thus its impossibility within actuality. However, as noted at the end of the last chapter, this impossibility must always be narrated in terms given by actuality.

This is a deepening of the problematic given in the first chapter, though transformed from its previous, speculative mode. There, the aporia of program and impulse resulted from utopia's inclusion and exclusion from actuality. Here, we discover that utopian narrative has its own version of this problematic, and we can confront the question of (non-)actuality directly since the concept of utopian narrative includes the actual, as prefiguration. Utopian narrative is prefigured by actuality, and so its narration of the impossible seems not to be truly impossible but only a particular configuration of the already-possible. I am drawn to this thought from Descartes' First Meditation:

> [E]ven when painters try to create sirens and satyrs with the most extraordinary bodies, they cannot give them natures which are new in all respects; they simply jumble up the limbs of different animals.[1]

Utopian narrative finds itself in a similar position. While we have escaped the attempt to imagine other worlds, utopian narrative needs to retain a sense of utopia's incompatibility with actuality if it is to remain truly utopian. The point of this chapter is to illustrate how utopian narrative can navigate this problematic.

Now, I should say something briefly about the modal categories at work in my argument, though a serious discussion on this topic does not have its place here. Given that the actual is typically opposed to the possible, my position that there is an aporia in the fact that utopia must be impossible, yet is only ever articulable in terms of what is possible, may seem to rest on the controversial premise that actuality implies possibility. While my argument may be compatible with this premise, it does not require it. Indeed, since I am working with the question of narrative, "actuality" refers to the field of human action that prefigures narrative configuration. What this configuration can represent as possible or impossible is thus dependent on actuality. Even something that appears totally impossible is only ever articulable on the basis of what prefigures it; so what appears totally impossible is, in a sense, what is *actually impossible*. If this is taken by the reader to be a contradictory category, then this would only strengthen my argument since it would belie the depth of the aporia that utopian narrative is forced to overcome. That said, I accept that I am unable to give sufficient discussion to these modal questions; I only hope that, since the relation between actuality and possibility is, here, a narratological one, I am able to avoid the murky waters of some more difficult questions regarding modal logic and metaphysics.

So far in my argument, the problems and their respective answers have been drawn from sources that are familiar to the study of utopia in modern European philosophy. However, at this point the argument appears to make a sharp turn toward another field, namely, that of black radical thought, in particular the work operating in the wake of Cedric Robinson's *Black Marxism*.[2] As I will note later, the idea of utopia makes several appearances in this field. However, for now I focus on showing that the aporia of (non-)actuality is also at work in the problematics investigated by Saidiya Hartman and Fred Moten, two central contemporary writers in "black studies".[3] This is oriented around what is basically a Spivakian question, namely, the question of how to represent what is, according to actuality, necessarily unrepresentable: "there is no access to the subaltern consciousness outside dominant representations of elite documents".[4] In Hartman's early work, this is a relatively moderate claim that could be applied to any number of struggles for liberation that have been mediated via an archive constructed by those with different experiences than those they are attempting to narrate. However, implicit here is the more radical question of how to relate slave narratives when so much of the history of how slaves were treated was simply not recorded. It is not merely that there is an epistemological problematic regarding how we are to relate a history that is always beyond both the archive and its narrativisation in the work of the historian; rather, the question is how to "narrat[e] stories which are impossible to tell".[5] For example, Hartman is concerned with telling the story of two girls who died aboard the *Recovery*: both had gonorrhoea, and both were put to death by the captain for it. We know some details of the death of one of these girls, due to a speech given in Westminster by William Wilberforce which brought about a trial of the captain for the murder.[6] But we know nothing of the other girl who was killed by the captain other than that she died and was called Venus by the others on the ship. This lack of knowledge which leads to the impossibility of telling Venus' story is no neutral fact, but it's "inseparable from the play of power that murdered Venus and her shipmate".[7] Therefore, this impossibility is a historical impossibility in the dual sense that it is impossible for the discipline of history to faithfully tell Venus' story, and also that this impossibility is the result of a historical process.

For Hartman, the imperative to try and tell Venus' story emerges from a feeling of debt, shown in her desire to retell the story as "a romance [of resistance] that exceeded the fictions of history" that was "unfettered by the constraints of the legal documents", so that it would appear to redeem Venus' suffering.[8] But since all attempts to recount her story will fail, Hartman chooses another path, which is to accept the contradictory status of her relation to Venus and, insofar as Venus operates as a synecdoche for much of the history of those who died under slavery, the rest of the object of her study. In attempting the necessarily failed project of retelling Venus' story, Hartman highlights the historical processes which have led to that impossibility, and subjects these processes to critique. Since they still operate today, she therefore critiques the present. But Hartman does not resolve the epistemological aporia, rather she attempts to "make visible the production of disposable lives [...], to describe 'the resistance of the object'", via the revelation of the impossibility of this telling.[9] This illustrates the failure of the promise that they might have lived such lives that would have produced stories that we could tell.

This is the problematic taken up by Fred Moten throughout his work, which finds its theoretical point of departure in the introduction to *In the Break*, titled, importantly, "Resistance of the Object". Moten begins in the same position as Hartman, by asking the question of how to tell the story of slavery in a way that would not be caught up in the discourses that contribute to the impossibility of this telling.[10] The problem is most explicitly stated in Moten's engagement with Fanon:

[I]f we cannot [...] give an account of things that, in the very fugitivity and impossibility that is the essence of their existence, resist accounting, how do we speak of the lived experience of the black?[11]

I will return to the question of how Moten and Hartman are able to draw the analysis of the conditions of the transatlantic slave trade to bear on "the black" in general. First, note that Moten begins by engaging with the epistemological problematic that animates Hartman's work, expressed in her refusal to reproduce the beating of Fredrick Douglass's Aunt Hester in favour of highlighting how frequently those scenes are reproduced in an instrumentalisation of the shocking spectacle.[11] In this scene, which marks Douglass's introduction to the reality of slavery, his Aunt Hester screams. This, Moten suggests, critiques Marx's analysis of the fetishism of the commodity in the opening chapter of *Capital Volume 1*. Crucial here is Marx's distinction between use-value and exchange-value. The former is just the capacity of any object to satisfy human needs, whereas the latter is the object's value in exchange with another. Exchange-value is presented as existing prior to all social relations, and so is the only real, objective value from the point of view of exchange. However, Marx argues that exchange-value as a social form only appears under particular historical conditions, namely, the capitalist mode of production, where labour is abstracted from concrete activity and paid per hour of labour-power provided. The *fetishism of the commodity* is thus the appearance that commodities have value insofar as they are objects independent of exchange, which they do not.

Here, Marx is using two discourses together that do indeed often come together, but are nonetheless distinct. One is the epistemological discourse of subjects and objects of knowledge, in the post-Kantian tradition of the subject being the condition of possibility for the representation of objects. The other is the opposition between person and thing, which is an ethico-legal discourse whereby persons have value such that they ought to be part of our moral considerations, whereas mere things do not have value. Generally, the human individual is both subject and person, as opposed to the objects of their knowledge, which are mere things. For Marx, if commodities really had value as a quality independent of exchange, then they would be persons, and if they were persons, then they would be humans and could thus speak. But commodities cannot speak; they are objects and thus mere things. So Marx has to, in a subjunctive mode, imagine what would be said "if commodities could speak". Apparently,

> they would say this: our use-value may interest men, but it does not belong to us as objects. What does belong to us as objects, however, is our value.[13]

Moten, in what seems like an obvious move, begins a critique of Marx "with the historical reality of commodities who spoke".[14] In contrast to commodities as understood by Marx, which are inanimate things raised to the appearance of value, slaves are *degraded persons*, reduced to the status of mere things.

Here, it is worth recounting Orlando Patterson's threefold description of slavery since it is so influential on Moten's argument. First, slaves are totally dominated such that they are no longer taken to be human, regarded as a mere thing with no will of their own; second, they are natally alienated, that is, there is no familial structure and thus their social relationships "were never recognised as legitimate or binding"; third, in combination of these two, slaves are always *dishonoured persons*; they, along with everything they are associated with, are taken to be entirely lacking in value.[15] But this is a reduction from something more, and it is a reduction that is resisted by Aunt Hester's scream and the scream of all other speaking commodities. Therefore, when slaves scream, not only does this scream challenge Marx's subjective silencing of the commodity, but it also is an assertion of what Marx says commodities would say if they could speak, which in Marx's analysis is a merely ideological assertion of the commodity's fetish-quality. The scream protests the slave's use by another, since their use-value under conditions of slavery is really only an accidental fact about the enslaved person, and it also asserts their essential value against the conditions which would reduce them to the status of mere things.

Despite operating in Hartman's wake, Moten's analysis appears to be less clearly related to the aporia Hartman identifies. However, when one recognises that the reduction to the status of a thing that the scream protests is the same reduction that resulted in Venus' execution and, indeed, the fact that her death went unrecorded, the argument becomes clearer. From the point of view of the exchange of human beings, the personhood of objects of exchange is impossible since they can only be submitted to the law of the market if they are reduced to mere things. For both Marx and capitalism, the commodity's speech is an impossible example since it is a resistance to actuality in its objection to the reduction to mere thingliness.

Moten's argument, however, goes even further:

[E]very approach to Marx's example must move through
the ongoing event that anticipates it, the real event of
the commodity's speech, itself broken by the irreducible
materiality […] of the commodity's scream.[16]

That is, when the commodity speaks, she does not speak in the manner that Marx subjunctively imagines that it might, but rather she *screams*. This sound is irreducible to any particular symbolic value, and yet it seems to possess a force that thereby challenges the Saussurean view that the value of a sign, its meaning, must be understood in abstraction from sound. That is, insofar as the meaning of terms is secured by their representational relations to other terms, a law of equivalence that establishes the value of the sign, the assertion of the value of the commodity is incommensurable with such a language. For now, I still want to leave aside the question of how Moten establishes that this is not a condition of a particular moment in the past, but is the historical condition of blackness today. Instead, note again that Moten has arrived at a similar problematic regarding how to narrate the impossible. If the value of the commodity, and indeed the value of the sign, is established in abstraction from the commodity's speech, then this scream is impossible to narrate on its own terms since the commodity's resistance can only be registered in terms of that which it resists. Hartman's problematic of how to confront the inadequacy of the historical archive is thus radicalised by Moten's argument that the resistance of the object is a materiality excluded from actuality that involves "a kind of temporal warp": what appeared as a historiographical symptom of racism and slavery now appears to be the general condition of these structures.[17] Still, whatever one thinks of Moten's argument that this is really the condition of slavery and, in the extension I have yet to make, blackness, it is clear that the aporia at work here is parallel to that of utopia. Indeed, I will make this extension by noting that blackness is not an ontological position but rather a historical narrative, constituted through those practices of remembrance that Hartman describes. Now, both Moten and Hartman want to argue that the resistance of the object is external to actuality insofar as it is anterior to the creation of the capitalist mode of production that constitutes this actuality. So, this resistance occupies the same position in their problematic as utopia does in my own, namely, that of a narrative which is always excluded by actuality but only ever articulable in terms of that actuality.

b. From Slavery to Blackness

Now, I want to argue that what is identified as "blackness" in this tradition is, in fact, utopian narrative. But to do so I must explain how this narrative of blackness functions. The crucial move is in Hartman's claim that what requires investigation is not the terror of the spectacle but rather that of "the mundane and the quotidian".[18] By this, Hartman means those everyday practices where domination and resistance are not so easily discernible, even the moments of apparent reprieve. For example, slaves' "Saturday night Dances", which might appear to be simply moments of play opposed to the domination of the working day, were nonetheless still overseen by the master in order to "cultivate contented subjection".[19] So, Hartman argues that certain practices which developed during slavery, and continued after its end in a way that the routinised beatings such as Hester's did not, form a tradition of clandestine practices of remembrance.[20] Naturally, these had to be clandestine, because any apparently autonomous action by the slave is a theft of the master's property. So, the songs that accompanied juba, a popular dance, "enacted resistance and aired dissent in the guise of play and sheer nonsense".[21] Thus, the liberatory force of such dances was not an affirmation free from domination, but was mediated by this domination: since slaves were excluded from personhood, this resistance was often viewed as mere nonsense. For example, shortly after the description of his Aunt's beating, Fredrick Douglass writes of the songs that "to many would seem unmeaning [but] were full of meaning to [the slaves]", but "every tone was a testimony against slavery, and a prayer to God for deliverance from chains".[22] Later, I will say a little more about the nature of this liberatory force; the point for now is to show that the resistance of the object is understood as the fundamental feature of social life under slavery: social life was conducted under the law that the slaves were not persons but things.

We have yet to connect this analysis of slave life to "blackness" more generally, especially as regards Moten's analysis. The important move for Moten occurs over the course of a short section in *Scenes of Subjection*, entitled "Performing Blackness". I quote an important sentence at length:

> [B]lackness is defined here in terms of social relationality rather than identity; thus blackness incorporates subjects normatively defined as black, the relations among blacks, whites, and others, and the practices that produce racial difference. Blackness marks a social relationship of dominance and abjection and potentially one of redress and emancipation.[23]

That is, "blackness" here refers to the process of devaluing that Moten describes and the speaking commodity resists, that reduces human beings to the status of mere things. The performance of blackness is the performance of this process of devaluing that results from natal alienation and domination. Thus begins the tradition of black performance that is the object of Moten's study in *In the Break*, as repetitions of this initial rupture from origins (not, I should add, an attempted return to a utopian Africa before slavery). Juba was not a re-enactment of a tradition handed down from generations in Africa, since the condition for the emergence of these practices is the destruction of the possibility of a search for origins in a romanticised past. At no point were the origins of juba clear: it has a possible etymology in various Bantu words; its features ranged from dancing, using the body as a percussive instrument, a song, and it could involve any number of people. Instead, juba is characterised by its use of repetition that testifies to the impossibility of telling a continuous narrative, given that the conditions that create slavery and, ultimately, the very existence of the category of blackness is the rupture from origins.[24] Insofar as blackness is a performance, it is formed on the basis of a tradition of rupture from origins, a tradition that says that tradition is impossible for blackness as such; it is the repetition for the sake of remembering this dishonouring reduction and the resistance to it.

I note at this point that this is the part of my argument that accords most with what, after Frank B. Wilderson III, has come to be known as "Afropessimism". That is, firstly, "Blacks are not Human subjects, but are instead structurally inert props"; secondly, that white supremacy, not private property as Marxism would have it, constitutes the "base" of society.[25] However, Wilderson's thesis is more radical than mine needs to be, so these two claims that differ from those of Patterson, Hartman and Moten need not be part of my argument, since I am concerned neither with the political or ontological priority of blackness over class, nor with the status of the human per se. Rather, I am arguing here, with Hartman and Moten, that the tradition of blackness emerges from the performance of the resistance of the object in clandestine and quotidian repetitions of this initial practice of rupture.

Given that what is called "blackness" in black studies occupies a subject position that I argued gives rise to the parallel aporia for utopia, it is remarkable that it is, on occasion, given precisely that name in this field. In a short piece, Stefano Harney, Fred Moten's collaborator, attempts to disavow a kind of romantic optimism regarding those moments of resistance I have discussed, the imagined space of which Moten and Harney call "the undercommons".[26] Specifically, however, this optimism is understood as a *utopianism*, where utopia is a "time and place" outside actuality "where we live together in peace and harmony".[27] While, for Harney, the undercommons is no utopia of this sort, it is nonetheless "historically impossible", since, in the production of sugar in the Caribbean, "slaves were not replaced by reproduction [...] but by more captured, stolen, and transported Africans".[28] The point, for Harney, is that the nature of the relation of blackness makes the idea of a black tradition, and thus of "blackness" as a historical condition, a kind of impossibility: non-persons are not, on this view, a part of "history" per se, except as passive things which are affected by events. Since blackness and utopia are both radically excluded from history, they share a modal relation to actuality; therefore, Harney declares that "blackness is the living utopia".[29] But though no one lives in utopia, the goodness of utopia means that everyone wants, or would want, to live there. This is not the case for the undercommons; it is only lived in by those who are forced there by a reduction to thingliness. Despite this reduction, however, life, community, and indeed tradition continue, at least in a clandestine form, which is impossible from the standpoint of actuality. Therefore, Harney concludes that "utopia is, in practice, no-thing at all", where this "no-thing" appears to have a kind of affirmative content; so blackness, as a tradition of persistence in the face of exclusion, is the nothing in actuality that belies the non-totality of that actuality.[30] What I want to do now is try to argue that, while dressed in a language that is specific to Harney and Moten's intellectual circle, this claim is grounded in previous work in the black radical tradition. Furthermore, I will explain a good deal more about the status of the "no-thing" here, which I will argue may be understood through Adorno's account of the subject and object.

Before doing this, I need to address a linguistic asymmetry between my work here and that of Moten and Harney. Frequently, their accounts of blackness are grounded in Derrida's deconstruction, in particular the concept of the supplement, as a kind of materiality that must be excluded from the representational relations of the symbolic function in order to serve as its ground. That is, the supplement is drawn from the outside of a binary opposition in order to produce the opposition, since the void between the terms, the absence of this supplement, is the condition of possibility of their opposition.[31] One reading of this work is to argue that blackness is the supplement to the opposition between person and thing. It is likely that Harney intends precisely this move, given that he grounds his argument in the modal discourse of blackness' impossibility which is at the same time necessary for the establishment of capitalism. As such, the supplementary character of that nebulous term *différance* "makes possible the very thing that it makes impossible", which means that in Derrida's analysis it occupies the same position as blackness in Harney's, understood as an aporia of necessity and impossibility rather than actuality and non-actuality.[32]

One might take issue with my non-attendance to this Derridean dimension of the argument. As stated in the previous chapter, I do not think that deconstruction permits the negativity required for an adequate account of utopian narrative in general, and, given that I am going to argue that what Moten identifies as "blackness" is really a particular instance of utopia, the identification of utopia with the supplement would bring me back into territory that I have already rejected. This would likely be worsened by the fact that the supplementary *différance* is often identified, in a utopian motif, as the condition for "the as yet unnameable which is proclaiming itself", meaning that my account would, once again, be remarkably similar to Derrida's.[33] Nonetheless, my use of Moten and Harney can be maintained for at least two reasons. One, my focus on Moten's early work, drawing only occasionally on the later work with and by Harney, allows me to take his early sympathy toward negative dialectics as espoused by Asha Varadharajan as a reason to read the object's resistance along the Adornian lines approached in the last chapter.[34] Two, as I argued earlier, the "impossibility" of blackness here just means a radical separation from actuality. There may be possibilities which are not a part of actuality, but they are not radically separated from it since they are *actually possible*. Utopia's radical separation from actuality amounts to an impossibility within the terms of that actuality.

As such, the apparent disjunction between my terminology and Harney's will require careful navigation, lest my account becomes problematically inconsistent with itself in affirming the potential of a utopian narrative rather than its negative relation to actuality, but there is no necessary inconsistency between my view here and Harney's.

c. Utopia and Resistance

I will return to the contemporary work in black studies that has so far dominated the discussion in this chapter. For now, I want to turn to some older writing in the black radical tradition. First, to one of the founders of the Black Panthers, Huey P. Newton. Newton's position in his major philosophical work, *Revolutionary Suicide*, is a kind of Marx-Nietzsche synthesis. His analysis of the workings of capitalism is thoroughgoingly Marxist, or rather dialectical materialist, influenced primarily by Mao. But, there, a specific reading of Nietzsche's will to power takes ontological precedence: "the will to power is the basic drive of man".[35] It is important to recognise what Newton means by this. It is no anthropocentric understanding of a drive in human beings but rather a force of nature in general. It is read with an expansion of Freud's concept of desire worthy of Deleuze and Guattari, so he responds to the question of "What is the will to power?" by answering that it is "the power of Eros the love force against the machines of death".[36] What Newton calls the will to power is, firstly, a power of resistance. Howard Caygill, in an important article, notes that the political practice of the Panthers was based around the organisation of this resistance, or at least the "capacity to resist".[37] I do not want to suggest that this is an especially Nietzschean concept, except insofar as, for Newton, the will to power, in fact, *is* this resistance within actuality which is prior to the creation of a particular actuality. Therefore, we see that the idea of resistance as understood by Fred Moten is prefigured in these writings by Huey P. Newton.

In another unpublished text entitled "Utopia: Universal Energy", Newton initially echoes the Marxist critique of utopia that he would have likely heard from Marcuse, that socialism is not a "utopia" in the traditional sense because thinking of it like this casts utopia into impossibility when, really, we should be saying that the conditions of actuality are making utopia a real historical possibility.[38] But throughout the text, Newton engages with the concept of the will to power, again as our power against domination. However, Newton then reads this concept of power onto that of *energy*, since "in nature", of which we are all a part, "power is energy".[39] Given this identification of (the will to) power with the capacity to resist, and utopia as that "universal energy" of nature, Newton submits that, in fact, utopia is the capacity to resist. Therefore, utopia is the resistance to actuality that is within actuality. It is worth quoting the concluding passage at length:

> We return to the concept of power and the Will to power
> which Freud, Adler, Nietzsche and Marx have redefined
> in our epoch. Now it is time to go on. Engels wrote that
> socialism is "based upon naturalism". It is nature that
> gives us a clue for survival. Power cannot much longer be
> taken out of nature; and political power without material
> or natural power is a cruel hoax; we know that very well in
> America today. But since nature in its essence is pure energy
> itself, and since we are an integral part of nature, for all of
> our famous alienation, our utopia is ~~not~~ nowhere and no
> place, it is *everywhere* and *everyplace*.[40]

This final line is striking in its similarity to Harney's formulation of utopia as the no-Thing within actuality, though it is universalised beyond the specific subject position of blackness. Here, Newton argues that this energy, utopia, the will to power, is in opposition to all the machines of death, but since that power is required by domination, it is also always a moment of utopian resistance.

Here, the concept of energy means something close to the post-Kantian category of actuality (*Aktus*), drawn from Aristotle's *energeia*, understood as "that which makes something happen".[41] Elsewhere, Newton understands domination as "the attempt of a few to seize on and control the energy of the many", so we should also understand energy as something similar to effort or, in another discourse, expenditure.[42] No doubt this concept of energy draws upon Freud's concept of psychic energy, which, again, is that which makes something happen (initially, a dream-thought).[43] In this case, this energy is a subterranean capacity that is the condition of possibility of actuality, where this actuality is that which, in Kant's formulation, "is connected with the material conditions of experience".[44]

This energy is required for our actuality but, as Newton notes, it is always resistant to the domination which has structured this field of action. So, capacity to resist in the subterranean is both required by and thus connected to actuality, but its resistance is also a negation of that actuality. Crucially, for Newton, the persistence of this resistance which occupies the aporetic relation to actuality, of both inclusion and exclusion, is the "universal energy" of utopia. Here, we are moving toward the view that utopian narrative is that of the constitutive resistance to any particular actuality.

A similar tendency is articulated in the opening chapter to Angela Davis' *Women, Race and Class*. In this essay, Davis appears, at first, to be simply correcting the historical record on the nature of black families in America against the myths of matriarchy, codified in the US's public record by the Moynihan Report. No doubt this is part of her project. However, another discourse, one of resistance and utopia, really governs the conceptual structure of the essay. Take the title itself, "The *Legacy* of Slavery: Standards for a *New* Womanhood": Davis's project is really in showing how familial relations and relations of reproduction under slavery might give us a clue to a non-patriarchal understanding of both womanhood and child-rearing.[45] That is to say, given the natal alienation that typified slavery, "the family", in the form it had come to take under capitalism, was not so much at work among slave communities.

Davis argues that domestic life had "exaggerated importance in the social lives of slaves, for it did indeed provide them with the only space where they could truly experience themselves as human beings".[46] Here, again, we have the subterranean persistence of (slave) life that Moten and Harney identify, against the machines of death that work toward its eradication. Being forced underground created conditions which necessitated new social formations, namely, the division of domestic labour, and indeed the abolition of a rigorous and hierarchal sexual division of that labour.[47] Here, resistance under conditions of slavery is narrated by Angela Davis in the 1980s to refigure experience in the present by illustrating, at least for a moment, the artificiality of the nuclear family. Again, the energy of resistance to domination which is required by actuality is really prior to that actuality and thus, when narrated by Davis, is the aporia within actuality itself.

Though the work of these two Panthers is exemplary of the tradition of utopian resistance that I want to identify, it is exemplified equally in the Afrofuturist tradition, particularly in the prose writings of Sun Ra. John Corbett argues that the mythic origins articulated in Ra's work again adopt natal alienation, this time an alienation from a home, as an opportunity to re-narrate this origin of blackness, to "mak[e] *this elsewhere* your own".[48] This means that Ra's connection to utopia, the narration of an origin that does not begin with domination but that is radically separated from actuality, should once again be understood within this tradition of utopian resistance as an aporia within actuality. That is, when Ra says, "I was not a product of the white world", this amounts to a declaration of a radical separation that is required by actuality.[49] There is a real declaration of other-worldliness here, but it is always, of course, mediated by the actuality that it resists. This is no defect, but rather establishes the critical potential of this resistance: indeed, utopias must be mediated by actuality in order to be articulable within it and, indeed, to retain their political force.

Therefore, the identification of utopia with this resistance long predates Moten and Harney's work. That said, the specific discourse of *nothingness* is, I suggest, rather new, and so the claim that this particular moment of the black radical tradition has bearing on my problematic requires explication. For Moten, the engagement with this concept comes, again, through the consideration of a normative aporia in black thought which, I submit, is an ethico-political consequence of the aporia of actuality and non-actuality. Broadly, the aporia is "between normativity and the deconstruction of norms".[50] This is, of course, a general problem: we need some normative standard drawn from actuality (justice, freedom, or whatever else) in order to indict the normative standards of actuality that we wish to escape. This aporia is played out in a debate between Moten and Jared Sexton, as representatives of "black optimism" and "Afropessimism", respectively. Moten appears to have greater optimism than Sexton and, indeed, Wilderson regarding the resistance of the object. Afropessimism, *contra* Moten, attempts to take a step back from normative prescription in favour of the description of a recognitive failure, the failure to see black social life as anything other than black social death.[51] Against this tendency, Moten is interested in lingering with this aporia rather than, as it might initially appear, merely opposing himself to the pessimism of his peers. For Moten, the question is to explain "how utopia came to be submerged in the interstices and on the outskirts of the fierce and urgent now", which thus requires thinking through the aporetic position of blackness as that which both resists and is required by actuality.[52] In practical terms, this amounts to the possibility of love for blackness, given that blackness is formed out of the reduction that it resists.[53] Wilderson assert that he is "nothing" in what is, it seems, a real rejection of all those values of normativity that one might standardly appeal to: freedom, equality, and everything else is refused in this refusal of even thingliness.[54] Moten's move is not to affirm instead that blackness is *something*, but to accept this nothingness and further "consider *what nothing is*".[55]

Moten's discourse here, and indeed my own, now appears to have shifted from the assertion of personhood that initially motivated the object's resistance. However, the claim here is only a deepening of that previous problematic. If the "personhood" from which the object is excluded is just as much bound up with the normativity that Moten, and indeed all liberatory politics, would want to reject, then the mere assertion of the personhood would be an affirmation of actuality, when really, the assertion must be the breaking of that actuality. Indeed, if the claim were merely that something normatively preferable within actuality was asserted, then this would have little relevance to my argument. Instead, for Moten, the problematic is of how this operating outside both personhood and thingliness can be narrated. For this purpose, Moten settles on the concept of nothingness, which it seems means much the same as what he was arguing in *In the Break*:

> We come from nothing, which is something misunderstood.
> It's not that blackness is not statelessness; it's just
> that statelessness is an open set of social lives whose
> animaterialized exhaustion remains as irreducible chance.[56]

This is a characteristically tricky passage from Moten, but, again, the point is that the nothingness here still grants the possibility of optimism, indeed a utopianism. In a phrase borrowed from Wilderson, Moten calls the condition of this optimism "fantasy in the hold", which is what is given by "the undercommon inheritance of another world".[57] Here, we are approaching a clear utopianism in Moten's own work, which joins Newton in holding that utopia is to be found in resistance to domination, in the energy that domination both requires and denies, so that Moten bears "the hope that blackness bears or is the potential to end the world".[58] This "nothingness" of blackness is, therefore, the resistant utopian energy described by Newton, and while it may well be caught up in some existential-phenomenological discourses via Fanon's reading of Sartre, the reading of "nothingness" can be isolated for my purposes. Certainly, it is *this* sense of nothingness that Harney refers to in that short essay which animates my investigation, and indeed is the one frequently used by Moten throughout his work. More so than Newton, Moten recognises that this energy cannot simply be described in terms of actuality; instead, it must be understood through a kind of narrative.

As a moment of pause, let me restate the position at which I have arrived. The aporia of (non-)actuality for utopian narrative, which went unanswered in the previous account of utopian memory, is mirrored in Hartman and Moten's work on the narrativisation of blackness. I have argued that, furthermore, there is a tradition of more explicitly utopian thought in black radicalism that involves the articulation of a social life that resists all of our actuality. In a final move, I now need to work this resistant utopianism together with the concept of utopian narrative at which I arrived in the previous chapter, which will transform both concepts such that I can respond to the aporia of actuality and non-actuality. For this, I turn back to Adorno and finally complete the argument I have been developing throughout this chapter.

d. What the Object Says

In returning to Adorno, this chapter has, in a sense, come full circle. Part of what motivates this return is that this concept of utopia located in the black radical tradition is remarkably similar to that found in Adorno's work. I hope that, after a reading of a few passages of *Aesthetic Theory* and some of Adorno's lectures, that will become clear. This raises the question of why I have not simply written this chapter on Adorno. Really, it is that the analyses of the concrete effectuations of the idea of utopia in black studies provide an illumination of the relation between utopia and actuality that Adorno failed in most cases to articulate. That said, I can start by noting that the ethical concept of resistance is most clearly elaborated in Adorno's lectures, *Problems of Moral Philosophy*, in response to precisely the same aporia of normativity in Moten's work, which I argued was a consequence of the aporia of (non-) actuality. Namely, that

> [w]e need to hold fast to moral norms [...] and at the same time to a sense of the fallibility of the authority that has the confidence to undertake such self-criticism.[59]

This is, interestingly, identified by Adorno as a Nietzschean problematic, and is answered in a manner that accords directly with Newton's prescription that "the good life today would consist in resistance to the forms of the bad life".[60] Anything other than this negative attitude would simply affirm the good life in terms of actuality, which must be overcome.

This concept of resistance emerges from Adorno's negative dialectics. I have no space here to elaborate the idea in great detail, but drawing out its general features will be sufficient. For Adorno, negative dialectics arise from the persistence of the non-identity of the concept and the object. For a set of concepts A and an object B, any predicative judgment that "A is B" will always be false since the particularity of B will always be in excess of the universality of the concept A; so, "the concept is always less than what is subsumed under it".[61] However, just as the object always exceeds the concept, a claim one might find in deconstruction, so the concept always exceeds the object, since the concept always "contains a pointer to something that goes well beyond" anything specific about the characteristics that are currently subsumed under that concept.[62] This antagonism, that the concept is always more than the object, and *vice versa*, is non-identity. However, the concept always identifies itself with its object insofar as its status as a concept is secured only by its reference to that object; so this contradiction between the concept and object is equally a contradiction within the concept itself. The playing out of these contradictions is dialectics, but since they produce no positivity, no unity of opposites, they are *negative* dialectics. This negativity prevents the object from ever being articulable within actuality, and the pretence that it could be articulated in actuality would amount to a claim that the actual is already utopia, which is none other than ideology, the assertion that we already live in the best of all possible worlds.

Despite positivity never being made actual, Adorno nonetheless recognises that declaring the falsity of the identification of concept and object requires the concept of truth, a kind of potential positivity. The irreconcilable depends on the promise of reconciliation, and this promise, this "motive force", is identified as utopia.[63] The promise, as we have seen, is articulated through the narrative of broken promises, the remembrance of the non-identity of concept and object, universal and particular. Indeed, for Adorno, the possibility of the concept achieving its truth, of corresponding to its object, would amount to a "utopia of cognition", the reconciliation of what is actually irreconcilable.[64] But since, as ideology, actuality presents itself as the true, the presentation of reconciliation within actuality is ideological. As such, we should say that "the ray of light that reveals the whole to be untrue is none other than utopia".[65] The object always resists enclosure under the concept, and this resistance is utopia.

I should clarify that the account of the promise at which I have now arrived entirely disallows the idea that the promises made to the oppressed of the past could be fulfilled. As such, my account moves beyond some of the more affirmative impulses in Benjamin's messianic philosophy of remembrance that was articulated in the previous chapter. We can no longer hold that utopian narrative's relation to actuality is a modification of the tradition of the oppressed that might complete their incomplete happiness, since this would presume that utopian narrative is not prefigured by this very oppression.[66] Instead, utopian narrative narrates a resistance to actuality from an illusory standpoint outside actuality. Here, I follow Adorno, who notes that while this standpoint is owed to the past (in agreement with Benjamin), it is also "utterly impossible" since it would always be "marked [...] by the same distortion and indigence which it seeks to escape".[67] Utopian narrative is that which comprehends the impossibility of its resistance within actuality while recognising the persistence of its impossible resistance to actuality.

I must now show how the object can perform this resistance. For Adorno, this is answered through the artwork, which, in its configuration of fragments in an apparent unity, appears to speak as if it were an autonomous subject. As such, it appears as an object that can act and a thing that has value. This much follows from my explanation of the memory of the artwork in the last chapter. However, in that chapter the contribution to utopian narrative was its relation to the promise. Here, however, I want to concentrate on what Adorno calls art's "linguistic" quality, since, insofar as this is the source of art's apparent subjectivity, it is a subjectivity born in objection, the resistant object found in Moten's work. For Adorno, what speaks in the artwork is not the artist but the artwork itself.[68] True, the artwork requires the labour of the individual artist in order to exist, but what is expressed is not this private I, but rather, by externalising the private in the socially mediated process of artistic production, the I finds its collective subject. Therefore, "it is a We that speaks and not an I".[69]

We should now say, firstly, that the process of reification is not the reduction of an object to pure non-conceptuality. Quite the opposite, since, following Marx, reification is the submission of all things under the single concept of exchange-value. Artworks, we need not to be reminded, are just as much subject to reification, but this reification is resisted by the speech of the artwork that, as I argued in the previous chapter, speaks the memory of accumulated suffering. Still, it resists precisely in the process of that reification, such that the artwork is really

> the expression of a social relation that bears in itself the law
> of its own reification: Only as things do artworks become
> the antithesis of the reified monstrosity.[70]

Only when artworks articulate the conditions of their reification, and so appear as if they were subjects, do they resist this reification. They do this, I should add, by pointing, in their form, to a value that is beyond exchange, that is not in actuality. Therefore, we move toward what is required to answer the aporia of (non-)actuality and something which sounds remarkably close to Moten's account of blackness. Artworks speak according to the law of reification, and are thus thoroughly actual, but by speaking the conditions of their existence, they appear to articulate meaning where there is none. As such, an artwork resists actuality by being thoroughly part of it: "a thing that negates the world of things".[71]

Now, this claim regarding the status of the artwork might appear to be a different question to the rather more epistemological one regarding the non-identity of the concept and object that moved us toward Adorno's work. However, the point is that the artwork's configuration allows it to articulate the irreconcilability of the object with actuality by representing an illusory moment of reconciliation whose falsity speaks of that reconciliation's exclusion from actuality. The speech of the artwork is, therefore, the speech of the non-actual, the negation of actuality. We are starting to truly resolve the aporia of actuality and non-actuality via the narrative operation of the artwork. The artwork's speech, the presentation of an illusorily reconciled totality, is irreducible to the concept and thus resists that concept's domination; but furthermore, the presentation of a value that is beyond exchange points toward a value which is not yet actualised, that is to say, it speaks of a good place radically separated from actuality: utopia.

The resistant object in Adorno is the artwork; for Moten, it is blackness, and its speech is the scream. Recall that "blackness", here, is not an ontological condition but rather a narrative of resistant objectivity that, in principle, can extend beyond the particular historical experience of African Americans that is relied upon in the literature following *Scenes of Subjection*. My point, which I hope is becoming clear, is that the reason the aporias of blackness parallel those of utopia is that they, in fact, refer to the same thing, a resistance to actuality within actuality, which can appear as non-actual only by an illusory moment supplied by a certain configuration. The rupture that utopian narrative articulates is always an illusory rupture, but it resists actuality precisely because of the merely illusory status of this rupture. For Moten, the scream of the speaking commodity, the tradition of which is the black tradition, proclaims a value beyond exchange but not yet actualised. That is to say, the object's speech does exceed domination by the process that makes her into an exchangeable thing; but in the scream, she also articulates the fact that she is being made a thing and, as such, expresses a value that is irreducible to exchange. Rather than merely belying the falsity of the totality of exchange, the scream presents a value that cannot be given to actuality and, like Adorno's artwork, thus speaks of utopia in its resistance to this actuality. The nothingness of blackness, this exclusion from actuality, is now revealed as the negation in Adorno's negative dialectics; it is the resistant work of the irreducibly material object against actuality's domination, but it is equally the illusory appearance of the application of existing concepts to objects to which they do not refer in actuality. So, we arrive at a re-working of *outopia*, the non-actuality of utopia, such that this no-place has become the resistance of the object as the resistance within actuality.

I want now to say a little more about how this fits with the concept of narrative that I have developed so far, which also requires further elaboration of the articulation of the resistance of the object. I will do this by way of an engagement with Moten's treatment of the photograph of Emmett Till's open casket. This, ultimately, will allow me to return to threefold mimesis and give a final account of utopian narrative that responds to this last aporia.

I need not repeat the story of Emmett Till's murder here, and so I will move more quickly to Moten's problematic. Given that, for Moten, blackness is defined by a *sound*, how can it be that the photograph of Till's ruptured face is able to articulate this sound? Here, we are approaching something like the question of the non-discursive language of the artwork in Adorno, insofar as this is a question of how something that cannot speak can appear to do so.[72] For Moten, looking at the photograph of Emmett Till involves a looking which "opens onto an unheard sound that the picture cannot secure but discovers", since looking at the photograph involves the memory of that which produced it.[73] No doubt, this remembrance was Till's mother's intention in leaving the casket open, in her performance. But, for Moten, and indeed surely for anyone, it is almost impossible to sustain looking at the photograph, not merely on account of the violence that it depicts but also of the violence that it remembers, at which we are compelled to look, from which our gaze always averts. Now, Moten argues, and I agree, that this produces a contradictory appearance of "a sound that is seemingly not there in this performance that this performance is about", and this sound is blackness, the speech of the object, utopia.[74] We must recall that this sound is irreducible to any symbolic value, since the speech of the object is a scream that proclaims a value outside exchange.

This is bound up with a question of political action: How was it that the photograph of Emmett Till "set in motion this nation's profoundest political insurrection and resurrection", a refiguration of experience such that a mass political resistance could take place?[75] For Moten, this is because the condition of possibility of the staging, taking, and publication of the photograph is a certain sound. The importance of figure of sound in Moten's work cannot be overstated, but since it is also caught up in a Derridean positivity that I want to avoid, we must be careful here. When Moten claims that Till's "photo and photographs in general bear a phonic substance", we need only draw from this that, in their configuration, photographs can appear to speak in a way that is irreducibly non-conceptual (or, as Adorno calls it, non-discursive), as if they were making sound. In the case of this photograph, what surrounds it is "a mourning whose rehearsal is also a refusal" of actuality, and this mourning is not presented, of course, in the photograph itself.[76] This mourning, for Moten, is a sound because it is the mourning, the remembrance of suffering and death, of a suffering that was protested with a scream. So, sound here is a figure of that which is incompatible with actuality, and since the remembrance of suffering in the photograph thus amounts to a narration of that sound, the photograph narrates its own impossibility within actuality. But just as the photograph, in being surrounded by a mourning, enacts a remembrance of the suffering of the past, it also makes this sound appear and thus produces a "shudder" in its listener that shudders at the memory of what caused the mutilation that Mamie Till displayed.[77]

The resistance of the object, therefore, penetrates the photograph as its sound. But this sound, we should remember, is always the result of a certain narrative configuration, such that it can make what is non-actual appear. The photograph's antagonism, between its mere visuality and the sound it appears to convey, makes it a living aporia of pessimism and optimism. The configuration of the narrative in this photograph allows "the antagonisms of society [to be] nevertheless preserved in it".[78] For Moten, blackness (or utopia) can only be represented artistically, and indeed only has the kind of political effect that Till's photograph could have, when the impossibility of its representation is itself represented, a narration of unreconciled life. Indeed, when Adorno writes, "art must testify to the unreconciled and at the same time envision its reconciliation; this is a possibility only for its nondiscursive language", he could have said "blackness" or "utopia" instead of art, and the statement would have held true.[79]

In this example of the photograph of Emmett Till, we have a model for utopian narrative that responds to the aporia of (non-)actuality. The photograph is prefigured by the history of racial violence and domination that led to Till's death and thus prefigured by Aunt Hester's scream. However, as I have already shown, since this domination always requires the resistance that opposes it, the prefiguration by a tradition of continuity is always accompanied by a ruptural tradition of resistance. The aporia that this chapter has been concerned with is really a configurative problematic. I traced a lineage of utopianism in the black radical tradition that understood the resistance that was both excluded from and necessitated by actuality as utopia. Out of Hartman and Moten's work, I showed that the narration of blackness, with its origin in exclusion, suffering and death, the alienation from origin itself, faced the same problematic. We are now in a position to say that utopian narrative can respond to the aporia of (non-)actuality by the narration of its aporetic position in actuality. Utopian narratives are thus still held to the standard of the debt to the suffering of the past, on account of the unfulfilled promise of reconciliation, but they will only do so, only be truly utopian, when they express the impossibility of fulfilling this debt, since the utopian narrative is configured in the actuality that it seeks to escape. The testimony of this irreconcilability is the speech of the commodity that is genuinely impossible to configure within actuality. Utopian narrative's debt to the past can only be truly fulfilled through the expression of the impossibility of this fulfilment.

So, utopian narrative will follow Mamie Till's configurative model and configure a memory that reveals to the present the unfulfilled promises of the past, but also the impossibility of that fulfilment. The commodity's speech presents the news from nowhere, but since nowhere is not a place, utopian narrative can only be utopian by narrating the aporia within actuality, and its appearance of reconciliation and rupture will always be merely illusory. Utopian narrative, configured from the standpoint of redemption, must narrate the history of resistance as an aporia within actuality, but in doing so will reveal its own condition of impossibility to be actuality itself, and, in appearing to nonetheless convey value and meaning, point to a value that lies beyond actuality, yet to be made actual.

This appearance only flashes up for a moment, but it is enough to refigure experience in shudder at actuality and turn energy in the present against the forces of actuality, the conditions of actuality's reproduction, those machines of death. Indeed, none of what has come in this chapter particularly changes the mode of utopian narrative's refiguration, but in answering the aporia of (non-)actuality, the utopian memory of domination and resistance produces a shudder at all of actuality. Not only is it revealed that the autonomous "I" was a semblance but also the non-actual, utopia as resistance, always accompanies any particular actuality such that this actuality is revealed to be a mere semblance. Therefore, utopian narrative reveals the whole to be untrue in all of its moments, narrating the impossibility of the non-actual within actuality. In Moten, this is the narration of blackness since blackness is the tradition of resistance to domination. But we can say, more generally, that this is the narration of utopia, the universal energy of resistance to all our actuality.

Chapter 3 Notes

[1] René Descartes, *Meditations on First Philosophy: With Selections from the Objections and Replies*, Rev. edn (Cambridge: Cambridge University Press, 1641 [1996]), p.13.

[2] Cedric J. Robinson, *Black Marxism: The Making of the Black Radical Tradition* (Chapel Hill, North Carolina: University of North Carolina Press, 1983 [2000]).

[3] Fred Moten, 'Black Op', *PMLA,* 123 (2008), 1743.

[4] Saidiya V. Hartman, *Scenes of Subjection: Terror, Slavery, and Self-Making in Nineteenth-Century America* (New York: Oxford University Press, 1997), p.10.

[5] Saidiya V. Hartman, 'Venus in Two Acts', *Small Axe: A Caribbean Journal of Criticism,* 12 (2008).

[6] Saidiya V. Hartman, *Lose Your Mother: A Journey Along the Atlantic Slave Route*, 1st edn (New York: Farrar, Straus and Giroux, 2007), p.142.

[7] Hartman, 'Venus in Two Acts', pp. 10–11.

[8] Ibid. p.9.

[9] Ibid. p.11.

[10] Fred Moten, *In the Break: The Aesthetics of the Black Radical Tradition* (Minneapolis: University of Minnesota Press, 2003), p.2.

[11] Fred Moten, 'The Case of Blackness', *Criticism,* 50 (2008), 187.

[12] Hartman, *Scenes of Subjection*, pp. 1–2.

[13] Karl Marx, *Capital Volume One* (London: Penguin, 1867 [1990]), p.176.

[14] Moten, *In the Break*, p.6.

[15] Orlando Patterson, *Slavery and Social Death* (Cambridge, Mass.: Harvard University Press, 1982), pp. 5, 7

[16] Moten, *In the Break*, p.12.

[17] Ibid. p.11.

[18] Hartman, *Scenes of Subjection*, p.4.

[19] Ibid. p.49.

[20] Ibid. p.4.

[21] Ibid.

[22] Moten, *In the Break*, p.21.

[23] Hartman, *Scenes of Subjection*, pp. 56–57.

[24] Ibid. p.75.

[25] Frank B. Wilderson, *Afropessimism* (New York: Liveright Publishing Corporation, a division of W.W. Norton and Company, 2020), p.15. Frank B. Wilderson, 'Gramsci's Black Marx: Whither the Slave in Civil Society?', *Social Identities,* 9 (2003), 225.

[26] Stefano Harney and Fred Moten, *The Undercommons: Fugitive Planning & Black Study* (Brooklyn, N.Y.: Minor Compositions, 2013).

[27] Stefano Harney, 'Undercommons and Utopia', in *A Poetics of the Undercommons,* ed. by Fred Moten (Sputnik & Fizzle, 2016), (p.3).

[28] Ibid.

[29] Ibid. p.4.

[30] Ibid.

[31] Jacques Derrida, *Of Grammatology*, 1st American edn (Baltimore: Johns Hopkins University Press, 1967 [1976]), p.145.

[32] Ibid. p.143.

[33] Jacques Derrida, 'Structure, Sign, and Play', in *Writing and Difference*, (London: Routledge, 1967 [2001]), (p.370).

[34] Asha Varadharajan, *Exotic Parodies: Subjectivity in Adorno, Said, and Spivak*, (Minneapolis: University of Minnesota Press, 1995). Moten makes explicit reference to this work in a lengthy footnote to the first sentence of *In the Break*, pp. 255–56 n1.

[35] Huey P. Newton, *The Huey P. Newton Reader* (Seven Stories Press, 2011), p.227.

[36] Huey P. Newton, 'Thoughts on the Will to Power', Box 40, Folder 2, Dr Huey P. Newton Foundation Inc. Collection, Green Library, Stanford University Libraries, 1978.

[37] Howard Caygill, 'Philosophy and the Black Panthers', *Radical Philosophy,* (2013), 10.

[38] Herbert Marcuse, *Five Lectures: Psychoanalysis, Politics, and Utopia* (London: Allen Lane, 1970). Huey P. Newton, 'Utopia: Universal Energy', Box 39, Folder 1, Dr Huey P. Newton Foundation Inc. Collection, Green Library, Stanford University Libraries, 1973; Newton, 'Thoughts on the Will to Power'

[39] Newton, 'Utopia: Universal Energy', p.5

[40] Ibid. p.11. My editions.

[41] Howard Caygill, 'Also Sprach Zapata: Philosophy and Resistance', *Radical philosophy*, 171 (2012), 22.

[42] Huey P. Newton, 'Energy and Aggression', Dr Huey P. Newton Foundation Inc. Collection, Green Library, Stanford University Libraries,1973, p.15.

[43] Sigmund Freud, *The Standard Edition of the Complete Psychological Works of Sigmund Freud*, 5 (London: Vintage Books, 1900 [2001]), p.506.

[44] Immanuel Kant, *Critique of Pure Reason* (Cambridge: Cambridge University Press, 1781 [1998]), A218/B266

[45] Angela Y. Davis, *Women, Race and Class* (London: Penguin Books, 1981 [2019]), pp. 1–25. My emphasis.

[46] Ibid. p.17.

[47] Ibid. p.14.

[48] John Corbett, *Extended Play: Sounding Off from John Cage to Dr. Funkenstein* (Durham, N.C.; London: Duke University Press, 1994), p.18. Author's emphasis.

[49] Sun Ra, *The Immeasurable Equation: The Collected Poetry and Prose* (BoD–Books on Demand, 2005), p.469.

[50] Moten, 'The Case of Blackness', p.178.

[51] Jared Sexton, 'The Social Life of Social Death: On Afro-Pessimism and Black Optimism', in *Time, Temporality and Violence in International Relations*, (Routledge, 2016), pp. 61–75 (p.36).

[52] Moten, 'Black Op', p.1746.

[53] Fred Moten, 'Blackness and Nothingness (Mysticism in the Flesh)', *South Atlantic Quarterly*, 112 (2013), 738.

[54] Frank B. Wilderson, *Incognegro: A Memoir of Exile and Apartheid* (Cambridge, MA: South End, 2008), p.265.

[55] Moten, 'Blackness and Nothingness (Mysticism in the Flesh)', p.741.

[56] Fred Moten, 'The Subprime and the Beautiful', *African Identities,* 11 (2013), 239.

[57] Moten, 'Blackness and Nothingness (Mysticism in the Flesh)', p.744.

[58] Ibid. p.739.

[59] Theodor W. Adorno, *Problems of Moral Philosophy* (Cambridge: Polity Press, 2000), p.169.

[60] Ibid. pp. 167–68.

[61] Theodor W. Adorno, *Lectures on Negative Dialectics: Fragments of a Lecture Course 1965/1966* (Cambridge: Polity, 2008), p.7.

[62] Ibid.

[63] Ibid. p.115.

[64] Adorno, *Negative Dialectics*, p.21.

[65] Theodor W. Adorno, *Hegel: Three Studies* (MIT Press, 1963 [1993]), p.88.

[66] Benjamin, *The Arcades Project*. N8,1

[67] Theodor W. Adorno, *Minima Moralia: Reflections on a Damaged Life* (London: Verso, 1951 [2005]), p.247.

[68] Adorno, *Aesthetic Theory*, p.227.

[69] Ibid. p.228.

[70] Ibid.

[71] Ibid. p.165.

[72] Ibid. p.231.

[73] Moten, *In the Break*, p.198.

[74] Ibid. p.200.

[75] Ibid. p.195.

[76] Ibid. p.199.

[77] Ibid.

[78] Adorno, *Aesthetic Theory*, p.229.

[79] Ibid.

POLITICAL AFTERWORD

Keep your mind in hell, and despair not.

There is a well-rehearsed demand on philosophy that it be effective. In the words of those granting funding for research, this is often understood as demanding that a work have "impact". This is, really, the reflection of the idea that a work of philosophy must be comprehensible, that I rejected in the foreword, which reduces a work to the extent to which it is already subsumed by actuality: if a work is judged primarily on its "impact", then the work is reduced to the extent to which it can work within our actuality.

This would be the destruction not only of philosophy but also of radicalism itself. One of the conclusions of my argument here is that utopian thought must remain steadfastly committed to its non-enclosure by whatever it is that it is trying to escape. I have also shown that such an escape will always be illusory, but it is this expression of the impossibility of a moment of escape that shows our actuality itself to be an illusion. But this means, still, that philosophy must not give up on itself, nor give up on utopia and thus reduce itself to mere practical impact.

There is, however, an accompanying demand, equally inescapable, that all this writing be something more than a game for those with postgraduate degrees to admire or disdain. There has to be something more than dialectical jousting (though perhaps this statement is mostly an expression of hope). Indeed, philosophy is nothing at all if it understands itself as totally without political import: philosophy is always a product of politics, so even philosophy which puts on a pretence of political abstention is, always, involved. As such, though the explanation of the "practicality" of philosophy is, to an extent, a momentary suspension of the philosophical, it must be part of philosophy lest this retreat into ideological speculation. No one wants to know how many angels can dance on the head of a pin.

Let me, then, say this. Herbert Marcuse, in his "Political Preface" to *Eros and Civilization*, argues that the conditions under which those in the Global North now live "are transforming the earth into hell". But this hell is concentrated in places away from the eyes of the citizens of Beverly Hills, Mayfair, and Monaco. It is those "infernal places" that "illuminate the whole".[1] I am uneasy about at least one aspect of Marcuse's argument here, namely, the invocation that the radical action of people of colour against colonialism and racial capitalism will do what white Westerners are too comfortable to bother with. That said, I will say that the inferno illuminates the whole. Those ways of life condemned to non-redemption, that are there primarily to be cured, are the inferno that will at first shine light on this whole before setting it ablaze.

Utopian narrative can be constructed in the articulation of these infernal identities, whose break with actuality will always be a falsehood and will show the whole to be false. Indeed, the point of such an inferno is not to hold those identities up as what is to be affirmed, what it is there that we can say "yes" to. The thought of utopia tells us that we do not live in the right world. We will not find liberation by excavating through the wreckage of history, no matter how hard we look. Utopia is not in history: it is not anywhere. Inferno illuminates the whole not because a revolutionary identity will emerge from its flames that will finally be the one to affirm: there is no redeeming a detention centre, there is no redeeming a prison. But in hell identity is at its most false, and, as such, at its most utopian.

So, just as this afterword has to appear as separate to philosophical analysis, so politics will always, for a moment, present itself as a break with society. Politics must always deny its comprehension from the point of the view of the whole, so denies its subsumption under the philosophical. Infernal identities are created by the machines of death and only secure their utopian quality by their negative relation to actuality. When one presents as outside of some system, outside of the wage-relation in structures of mutual aid, outside of gender in non-binary expression, in fugitive defiance of race as a determining force, all these are false. But they are no more false than what is given.

It is hard work to maintain an illusion: the machines of death know this. So we infernals must work harder. Keeping up the apparition of the non-actual within the actuality is a battle, and like other battles, this one will be won by an organised mass. Leaning too far into a strategy of individuality, believing that by making oneself smaller one will be less easily engulfed by the rest of actuality, is always a mistake: we are always part of actuality. The illusion will only ever be maintained with collective support.

Still, this is not a battle that can be won in the open, but it can be won by a guerrilla infernality that knows hell better than its enemy. It must stay out of sight, and when it is seen it will never appear as itself, since it never can. At each moment, the enemy will try to find truth in inferno's flames; it will look for something to affirm. But inferno's strength is in never letting them know what it is, because it cannot be. Radical politics can only occur as the suspension of what is.

Utopian narrative articulates an impossibility, the non-actual within the actual. That is why radical politics must cling to utopia. We must not fall into the defense of an identity, absolutely opposed to the machines of death, that will in the last instance become a part of the machine we seek to oppose. Nor can we condemn these as mere falsehoods in comparison to a more real, more material struggle. Of course we live in the false: falsehood is all there is! Utopian narrative articulates the necessity of the non-actual within the actual, dissolving the actual with a solution of its own creation.

Mark Fisher writes that "for now, our desire is nameless", in hoping for a label to attribute to the political movement that would come in the 21st century to truly break with the 20th. He is right that whatever organises our politics is nameless, but wrong that it will have a name or, indeed, could ever be named. The name of utopia is nothing, and nothing cannot be said. Our politics is the falsehood of all naming, of all actuality. It will not be found in a heaven, and we ought not hope for a desire to save us: it is not coming. Utopia is found only in hell. So we must live there. Nothing can save us now.

Notes
[1] Marcuse, *Eros and Civilization*, xiii

BIBLIOGRAPHY

Miguel Abensour, 'Persistent Utopia', *Constellations,* 15 (2008).

Theodor W. Adorno, *Minima Moralia: Reflections on a Damaged Life,* trans. E. F. N. Jephcott, *Radical Thinkers* (London: Verso, 1951 [2005]).

———, *Hegel: Three Studies* (MIT Press, 1963 [1993]).

———, 'On Tradition', *Telos,* 1992 (1966 [1992]), 75–82.

———, *Negative Dialectics,* trans. Dennis Redmond (1966 [2001]).

———, *Aesthetic Theory* (London: Bloomsbury Academic, 1970 [2014]).

———, *Ästhetische Theorie* (Berlin: De Gruyter, 1970 [2021]).

———, *Problems of Moral Philosophy,* trans. Rodney Livingstone (Cambridge: Polity Press, 2000).

———, *Lectures on Negative Dialectics: Fragments of a Lecture Course 1965/1966* (Cambridge: Polity, 2008).

Amanda Beech, Robin Mackay, and James Wiltgen, *Construction Site for Possible Worlds* (Cambridge, MA: MIT Press, 2020).

Walter Benjamin, *Origin of the German Trauerspiel,* trans. Howard Eiland (Cambridge, MA; London: Harvard University Press, 1928 [2019]).

———, 'Paris, the Capital of the Nineteenth Century', in *The Arcades Project,* ed. by Rolf Tiedemann, trans. Howard Eiland and Kevin McLaughlin (Cambridge, Massachusetts; London: Belknap Press, 1935 [1999]).

———, 'The Storyteller', in *Illuminations,* ed. by Hannah Arendt (London: Fontana, 1936 [1973]).

———, 'The Work of Art in the Age of Mechanical Reproduction', in *Illuminations*, ed. by Hannah Arendt, trans. Harry Zohn (London: Fontana, 1936 [1973]).

———, 'On Some Motifs in Baudelaire', in *Illuminations*, ed. by Hannah Arendt, (London: Fontana, 1939 [1973]).

———, 'Theses on the Philosophy of History', in *Illuminations*, ed. by Hannah Arendt, trans. Harry Zohn (London: Fontana, 1940 [1973]).

———, *The Arcades Project*, trans. Howard Eiland and Kevin McLaughlin (Cambridge, Mass.; London: Belknap Press, 1982 [1999]).

———, *The Correspondence of Walter Benjamin, 1910–1940*, trans. Manfred R. Jacobson and Evelyn M. Jacobson (Chicago; London: University of Chicago Press, 1994).

Ernst Bloch, *The Spirit of Utopia*, trans. Anthony A. Nassar (Stanford, Calif.: Stanford University Press; Cambridge: Cambridge University Press, 1918 [2000]).

———, *Erbschaft Dieser Zeit* (Frankfurt am Main: Suhrkamp Verlag, 1935).

———, *Heritage of Our Times*. trans. Neville Plaice and Stephen Plaice (Oxford: Polity, 1935 [1990]).

———, *The Principle of Hope*, trans. Neville Plaice, Stephen Plaice and Paul Knight. Vol. 1 (Oxford: Basil Blackwell, 1954 [1986]).

———, *The Utopian Function of Art and Literature: Selected Essays*, trans. Alan Bass (MIT Press, 1989).

Susan Buck-Morss, *Dialectics of Seeing: Walter Benjamin and the Arcades Project, Studies in Contemporary German Social Thought* (Cambridge, Mass; London: MIT Press, 1989).

Howard Caygill, 'Also Sprach Zapata: Philosophy and Resistance', *Radical philosophy*, 171 (2012).

———, 'Philosophy and the Black Panthers', *Radical Philosophy* (2013), 7–13.

John Corbett, *Extended Play: Sounding Off from John Cage to Dr. Funkenstein* (Durham, N.C.; London: Duke University Press, 1994).

Angela Y. Davis, *Women, Race and Class, Penguin Modern Classics* (London: Penguin Books, 1981 [2019]).

Jacques Derrida, *Of Grammatology*, trans. Gayatri Chakravorty Spivak. 1st American edn (Baltimore: Johns Hopkins University Press, 1967 [1976]).

——, 'Structure, Sign, and Play', in *Writing and Difference* (London: Routledge, 1967 [2001]).

——, *Specters of Marx: The State of the Debt, the Work of Mourning, and the New International*, trans. Peggy Kamuf (New York; London: Routledge, 1993 [2006]).

——, 'Marx and Sons', in *Ghostly Demarcations: A Symposium on Jacques Derrida's Spectres of Marx*, ed. by Michael Sprinker, trans. G.M. Goshgarian, (London: Verso, 1999 [2008]).

René Descartes, *Meditations on First Philosophy: With Selections from the Objections and Replies,* trans. John Cottingham. Rev. edn, *Cambridge Texts in the History of Philosophy* (Cambridge: Cambridge University Press, 1641 [1996]).

Charles Fourier, *The Theory of the Four Movements.* trans. Ian Patterson, *Cambridge Texts in the History of Political Thought* (Cambridge: Cambridge University Press, 1808 [1996]).

——, *The Utopian Vision of Charles Fourier: Selected Texts on Work, Love and Passionate Attraction,* trans. Jonathan Beecher and Richard Bienvenu (London: J. Cape, 1972).

Sigmund Freud, *The Standard Edition of the Complete Psychological Works of Sigmund Freud,* trans. James Strachey, Anna Freud, Alix Strachey and Alan Tyson, ed. by James Strachey. 24 vols. Vol. 5 (London: Vintage Books, 1900 [2001]).

Stefano Harney, 'Undercommons and Utopia', in *A Poetics of the Undercommons*, ed. by Fred Moten (Sputnik & Fizzle, 2016).

Stefano Harney and Fred Moten, *The Undercommons: Fugitive Planning & Black Study* (Brooklyn, N.Y.: Minor Compositions, 2013).

Saidiya V. Hartman, *Scenes of Subjection: Terror, Slavery, and Self-Making in Nineteenth-Century America, Race and American Culture* (New York: Oxford University Press, 1997).

——, *Lose Your Mother: A Journey Along the Atlantic Slave Route.* 1st edn (New York: Farrar, Straus and Giroux, 2007).

————, 'Venus in Two Acts', *Small Axe: A Caribbean Journal of Criticism,*
12 (2008), 1–14.

Georg Wilhelm Friedrich Hegel, *The Phenomenology of Spirit,* trans. Terry
P. Pinkard, *The Cambridge Hegel Translations* (Cambridge: Cambridge
University Press, 1807 [2018]).

Martin Heidegger, *Being and Time,* trans. Edward S. Robinson and John
Macquarrie (San Francisco: Harper and Row, 1927 [1962]).

Peter Hudis, *Marx's Concept of the Alternative to Capitalism, Historical
Materialism Book Series* (Leiden; Boston: Brill, 2012).

Fredric Jameson, 'Reification and Utopia in Mass Culture', *Social text* (1979),
130–48.

————, 'Future City', *New Left Review,* 21 (2003).

————, 'The Politics of Utopia', *New Left Review,* 25 (2004), 19.

————, *Archaeologies of the Future: The Desire Called Utopia and Other
Science Fictions* (London: Verso, 2005).

————, *Valences of the Dialectic* (London: Verso, 2009).

Immanuel Kant, *Critique of Pure Reason,* trans. Paul Guyer and Allen W.
Wood, *The Cambridge Edition of the Works of Immanuel Kant* (Cambridge:
Cambridge University Press, 1781 [1998]).

————, 'Groundwork for the Metaphysics of Morals', in *Practical Philosophy,*
ed. by Mary J. Gregor, trans. Mary J. Gregor (Cambridge: Cambridge
University Press, 1785 [1999]).

David Leopold, 'On Marxian Utopophobia', *Journal of the History of
Philosophy,* 54 (2016), 111–34.

Herbert Marcuse, 'Contributions to a Phenomenology of Historical
Materialism', in *Heideggerean Marxism,* ed. by John Abromeit and
Richard Wolin, trans. Eric Oberle (Lincoln, NE: University of Nebraska
Press, 1928 [2005]).

————, *Eros and Civilization: A Philosophical Inquiry into Freud* (London:
Allen Lane, The Penguin Press, 1955 [1969]).

————, *Five Lectures: Psychoanalysis, Politics, and Utopia* (London: Allen
Lane, 1970).

Karl Marx, 'The 18th Brumaire of Louis Bonaparte', in *Marx and Engels:
Collected Works V. 11,* ed. by Maurice Cornforth, E.J. Hobsbawm,
Nicholas Jacobs, Margaret Mynatt, Salo Ryazanskaya, Lydia Belyakova,

Victor Schnittke and Norire Ter-Akopyan, trans. Clemens Dutt, Rodney Livingstone and Christopher Upward (London: Lawrence & Wishart, 1852 [2010]).

———, *Capital Volume One*, trans. Ben Fowkes, *Penguin Classics* (London: Penguin, 1867 [1990]).

———, 'The Civil War in France', in *Karl Marx: Selected Writings*, ed. by David McLellan, (Oxford: Oxford University Press, 1871 [2000]).

———, 'Political Indifferentism', in *The Political Writings* (London; New York: Verso, 1873 [2019]).

Karl Marx and Friedrich Engels, 'The Communist Manifesto', in *Karl Marx: Selected Writings*, ed. by David McLellan (Oxford: Oxford University Press, 1848 [2000]).

———, 'The Alleged Splits in the International', in *The Political Writings* (London; New York: Verso, 1872 [2019]).

John McCole, *Walter Benjamin and the Antinomies of Tradition* (Ithaca; London: Cornell University Press, 1993).

Thomas More, *Utopia*, trans. Robert M. Adams, third ed., *Cambridge Texts in the History of Political Thought* (Cambridge: Cambridge University Press, 1551 [2016]).

Fred Moten, *In the Break: The Aesthetics of the Black Radical Tradition* (Minneapolis: University of Minnesota Press, 2003).

———, 'Black Op', *PMLA,* 123 (2008), 1743–47.

———, 'The Case of Blackness', *Criticism,* 50 (2008), 177–218.

———, 'Blackness and Nothingness (Mysticism in the Flesh)', *South Atlantic Quarterly,* 112 (2013), 737–80.

———, 'The Subprime and the Beautiful', *African Identities,* 11 (2013), 237–45.

Huey P. Newton, 'Energy and Aggression', in *Dr Huey P. Newton Foundation Inc. Collection*, ed. by Stanford University Libraries (Green Library, 1973).

———, 'Utopia: Universal Energy', in *Dr Huey P. Newton Foundation Inc. Collection*, ed. by Stanford University Libraries (Green Library, 1973).

———, 'Thoughts on the Will to Power', in *Dr Huey P. Newton Foundation Inc. Collection*, ed. by Stanford University Libraries (Green Library, 1978).

————, *The Huey P. Newton Reader* (Seven Stories Press, 2011).

Fumi Okiji, *Jazz as Critique: Adorno and Black Expression Revisited* (Stanford, California: Stanford University Press, 2018).

Peter Osborne, *The Politics of Time: Modernity and Avant-Garde* (London: Verso, 1995).

————, 'The Dreambird of Experience: Utopia, Possibility, Boredom', *Radical philosophy*, 137 (2006).

————, 'Theorem 4: Autonomy: Can It Be True of Art and Politics at the Same Time?', *Open: Cahier on Art and the Public Domain*, 23 (2012), 116–26.

————, 'Out of Sync: Tomba's Marx and the Problem of a Multi-Layered Temporal Dialectic', *Historical Materialism*, 23 (2015), 39–48.

Orlando Patterson, *Slavery and Social Death, A Comparative Study* (Cambridge, Mass.: Harvard University Press, 1982).

Sun Ra, *The Immeasurable Equation: The Collected Poetry and Prose* (BoD–Books on Demand, 2005).

Paul Ricœur, *Time and Narrative*. Vol. 1 (Chicago: University of Chicago Press, 1984).

————, *Time and Narrative*. Vol. 2 (Chicago; London: University of Chicago Press, 1985).

————, *Lectures on Ideology and Utopia*, trans. George H. Taylor (New York: Columbia University Press, 1986).

————, *Time and Narrative*. Vol. 3 (Chicago; London: University of Chicago Press, 1988).

————, *Memory, History, Forgetting* (Chicago: University of Chicago Press, 2004), pp. xvii, 642 pages.

Cedric J. Robinson, *Black Marxism: The Making of the Black Radical Tradition* (Chapel Hill, North Carolina: University of North Carolina Press, 1983 [2000]).

Ernest G Schachtel, 'On Memory and Childhood Amnesia', *Psychiatry*, 10 (1947), 1–26.

Fredric J. Schwartz, 'Ernst Bloch and Wilhelm Pinder: Out of Sync', *Grey Room* (2001), 55–89.

Jared Sexton, 'The Social Life of Social Death: On Afro-Pessimism and Black Optimism', in *Time, Temporality and Violence in International Relations* (Routledge, 2016), pp. 61–75.

Peter Thompson, 'Introduction', in *The Privatization of Hope: Ernst Bloch and the Future of Utopia, SIC 8*, ed. by Peter Thompson and Slavoj Žižek (Durham, NC: Duke University Press, 2013).

Peter Thompson and Slavoj Žižek, *The Privatization of Hope: Ernst Bloch and the Future of Utopia, SIC 8* (Durham: Duke University Press, 2013).

Asha Varadharajan, *Exotic Parodies: Subjectivity in Adorno, Said, and Spivak* (Minneapolis: University of Minnesota Press, 1995).

Frank B. Wilderson, 'Gramsci's Black Marx: Whither the Slave in Civil Society?', *Social Identities*, 9 (2003), 225–40.

——, *Incognegro: A Memoir of Exile and Apartheid* (Cambridge, MA: South End, 2008).

——, *Afropessimism* (New York: Liveright Publishing Corporation, a division of W.W. Norton and Company, 2020).

CULTURE, SOCIETY & POLITICS

Contemporary culture has eliminated the concept and public figure of the intellectual. A cretinous anti-intellectualism presides, cheer-led by hacks in the pay of multinational corporations who reassure their bored readers that there is no need to rouse themselves from their stupor. Zer0 Books knows that another kind of discourse — intellectual without being academic, popular without being populist — is not only possible but already flourishing. Zer0 is convinced that in the unthinking, blandly consensual culture in which we live, critical and engaged theoretical reflection is more important than ever before.
If you have enjoyed this book, why not tell other readers by posting a review on your preferred book site.
You may also wish to
subscribe to our Zer0 Books YouTube Channel.

Bestsellers from Zer0 Books include:

Poor but Sexy
Culture Clashes in Europe East and West
Agata Pyzik
How the East stayed East and the West stayed West.
Paperback:978-1-78099-394-2 ebook: 978-1-78099-395-9

An Anthropology of Nothing in Particular
Martin Demant Frederiksen
A journey into the social lives of meaninglessness.
Paperback: 978-1-78535-699-5 ebook: 978-1-78535-700-8

In the Dust of This Planet
Horror of Philosophy vol. 1
Eugene Thacker
In the first of a series of three books on the Horror of Philosophy,
In the Dust of This Planet offers the genre of horror as a way of
thinking about the unthinkable.
Paperback: 978-1-84694-676-9 ebook: 978-1-78099-010-1

The End of Oulipo?
An Attempt to Exhaust a Movement
Lauren Elkin, Veronica Esposito
Paperback: 978-1-78099-655-4 ebook: 978-1-78099-656-1

Capitalist Realism
Is There No Alternative?
Mark Fisher
An analysis of the ways in which capitalism has presented itself
as the only realistic political-economic system.
Paperback: 978-1-84694-317-1 ebook: 978-1-78099-734-6

Rebel Rebel
Chris O'Leary
David Bowie: every single song. Everything you want to know,
everything you didn't know.
Paperback: 978-1-78099-244-0 ebook: 978-1-78099-713-1

Cartographies of the Absolute
Alberto Toscano, Jeff Kinkle
An aesthetics of the economy for the twenty-fi rst century.
Paperback: 978-1-78099-275-4 ebook: 978-1-78279-973-3

Malign Velocities
Accelerationism and Capitalism
Benjamin Noys
Long listed for the Bread and Roses Prize 2015, *Malign Velocities*
argues against the need for speed, tracking acceleration
as the symptom of the ongoing crises of capitalism.
Paperback: 978-1-78279-300-7 ebook: 978-1-78279-299-4

Babbling Corpse
Vaporwave and the Commodifi cation of Ghosts
Grafton Tanner
Paperback: 978-1-78279-759-3 ebook: 978-1-78279-760-9

New Work New Culture
Work we want and a culture that strengthens us
Frithjof Bergmann
A serious alternative for humankind and the planet.
Paperback: 978-1-78904-064-7 ebook: 978-1-78904-065-4

Romeo and Juliet in Palestine
Teaching Under Occupation
Tom Sperlinger
Life in the West Bank, the nature of pedagogy and the role of a
university under occupation.
Paperback: 978-1-78279-637-4 ebook: 978-1-78279-636-7

Color, Facture, Art and Design
Iona Singh
This materialist definition of fine art develops guidelines for
architecture, design, cultural studies, and ultimately, social
change.
Paperback: 978-1-78099-629-5 ebook: 978-1-78099-630-1

How to Dismantle the NHS in 10 Easy Steps (Second Edition)
Youssef El-Gingihy
The story of how your NHS was sold off and why you will have
to buy private health insurance soon. A new expanded second
edition with chapters on junior doctors' strikes and government
blueprints for US-style healthcare.
Paperback: 978-1-78904-178-1 ebook: 978-1-78904-179-8

Digesting Recipes
The Art of Culinary Notation
Susannah Worth
A recipe is an instruction, the imperative tone of the expert, but
this constraint can offer its own kind of potential. A recipe need
not be a domestic trap but might instead offer escape —
something to fantasise about or aspire to.
Paperback: 978-1-78279-860-6 ebook: 978-1-78279-859-0

Most titles are published in paperback and as an ebook.
Paperbacks are available in traditional bookshops. Both print
and ebook formats are available online.
Follow us at:
https://www.facebook.com/ZeroBooks
https://twitt e.rcom/Zer0Books
https://www.instagram.com/zero.books

For video content, author interviews and more, please subscribe to our YouTube channel:

zer0repeater

Follow us on social media for book news, promotions and more:

Facebook: ZeroBooks

Instagram: @zero.books

Twitter: @Zer0Books

Tik Tok: @zer0repeater